President Bush

The Challenge Ahead

President Bush

The Challenge Ahead

Congressional Quarterly Inc.
1414 22nd Street N.W.
Washington, D.C. 20037

Congressional Quarterly Inc.

Congressional Quarterly Inc., an editorial research service and publishing company, serves clients in the fields of news, education, business, and government. It combines Congressional Quarterly's specific coverage of Congress, government, and politics with the more general subject range of an affiliated service, Editorial Research Reports.

Congressional Quarterly publishes the *Congressional Quarterly Weekly Report* and a variety of books, including college political science textbooks under the CQ Press imprint and public affairs paperbacks on developing issues and events. CQ also publishes information directories and reference books on the federal government, national elections, and politics, including the *Guide to Congress,* the *Guide to the U.S. Supreme Court,* the *Guide to U.S. Elections, Politics in America,* and *Congress A to Z: CQ's Ready Reference Encyclopedia.* The *CQ Almanac,* a compendium of legislation for one session of Congress, is published each year. *Congress and the Nation,* a record of government for a presidential term, is published every four years.

CQ publishes the *Congressional Monitor,* a daily report on current and future activities of congressional committees, and several newsletters including *Congressional Insight,* a weekly analysis of congressional action, and *Campaign Practices Reports,* a semimonthly update on campaign laws.

An electronic online information system, Washington Alert, provides immediate access to CQ's databases of legislative action, votes, schedules, profiles, and analyses.

RECEIVED

OCT 3 1 1989

**Kennedy School
Library**

Library of Congress Cataloging-in-Publication Data

President Bush: the challenge ahead.
    p.   cm.
   Includes index.
   ISBN 0-87187-512-8:
   1. United States--Politics and government--1989- 2. Bush, George,
1924- . I. Congressional Quarterly, Inc.
E881.P74 1989
973.928'092--dc20

89-31458
CIP

Table of Contents

1

Taking Charge of Divided Government

George Bush, the nation's forty-first president, took office January 20, 1989, fresh from a decisive election victory at the head of the national Republican ticket. But he faced a Congress whose Democratic majority had actually been enlarged by the November voting. The electorate had spoken with a forked tongue, opting for a continuation of divided government.

Bush and his running mate, Sen. Dan Quayle of Indiana, captured 53.4 percent of the vote and carried forty states, rolling up 426 of the 538 electoral votes. However, it was an election that featured a 50.1 percent voter-turnout rate, the lowest since 1924. Only half of the American people old enough to vote actually cast a ballot in the 1988 presidential election. Measured against the entire voting-age population of more than 182 million, Bush was the choice of barely one out of every four adult Americans. Other presidents have been the choice of a smaller share of the entire electorate than Bush—including Harry S Truman in 1948, Richard Nixon in 1968, and even Ronald Reagan in 1980. But all three had third-party opposition that drained votes from their total. And all three could point to gains for their party in at least one house of Congress.

The national mood as expressed by the election's low turnout and actual results muddled all attempts to discern which party's vision of America would serve as the governing outlook for the nation, and who would hold a leadership mandate to deal with a daunting list of "Things to Do." It was a backlogged agenda of substantive issues carried over from the Reagan administration and addressed only superficially in the 1988 election campaign by either major-party candidate.

President Bush inherited a $150 billion federal budget deficit that required painful choices about spending and taxes. Since year-by-year deficit reductions were required by law, and the president persistently vowed not to raise taxes, the choices focused essentially on what priorities to assign a host of defense and domestic programs. After a massive arms buildup in Reagan's first term, military spending had slumped under the impact of federal budget constraints, requiring Bush and his defense chiefs to decide where to cut costs without sacrificing national security.

From his long Washington experience, Bush should not have been surprised that his country's clout in the world was being limited by the government's pocketbook. He ran square into the contradictory legacies of the Reagan era: renewed U.S. global activism and diminished resources to follow through on that activism. Ronald Reagan's

1

Whose Mandate?

A mandate seems to be in the eye of the beholder. The day after the election, President Reagan praised George Bush and Dan Quayle "for going to the people ... and asking for a mandate on critical matters like taxing and spending power, the nature of judiciary appointments, the strength of our defenses, and the firmness of our foreign policy." That mandate, Reagan continued, "has been unmistakably delivered."

But the defeated Democratic presidential candidate, Michael S. Dukakis, dismissed the idea of a Republican mandate in light of the voters' decision to return a Democratic-controlled Congress.

"Bush starts with a very fragile mandate," said Curtis B. Gans, director of the the Center for the Study of the American Electorate. Everett C. Ladd, director of the Roper Center for Public Opinion Research, said Bush's mandate rests in the fact that Republicans have won five of the last six presidential elections. "There has been some declaration on the part of the electorate," Ladd said. "It's real and purposeful, not a short-term reaction to negative ads. . . ."

The mandate question was perhaps best put in perspective by John F. Kennedy. According to Washington folklore, soon after he was elected president, reporters asked him whether his narrow margin of victory left him without a mandate to govern. Kennedy supposedly replied: "Mandate, 'schmandate.' I'm on this side of the desk and you're on that side."

tenure increased public expectations of the presidency, yet political scholars insisted that Congress—not the White House—had continued to gain power.

Pragmatism Replaces Ideology

As for the new president, he came into office emphasizing pragmatism instead of ideology, and bipartisan teamwork instead of confrontation. Bush said he wanted to be "president of all the American people," and looked for ways to get as close to them as possible. He took the oath not in formal attire but in a plain business suit. He popped out of his limousine to walk portions of the inaugural parade route. And all comers were invited to a White House reception the next day—the first such invitation in eighty years.

In his inaugural address from the Capitol's grand West Portico, Bush referred to it as one great front porch, "a good place to talk as neighbors, and as friends." On the whole, the twenty-minute address sought to please both those preferring a pragmatic statement and those listening for a crusader's hymn.

Bush and his transition team had worked since Election Day to convey a set of political messages. While his post-election remarks and appointments conveyed the firm notion that the new administration would be different from Reagan's, the inaugural planners took pains to portray continuity as well as change. George and Barbara Bush remained deferential to Ronald and Nancy Reagan; the departing Reagans seemed in no sense deposed. Boarding a helicopter at the Capitol's East Front for the trip back to California, the outgoing president paused at the chopper's door and saluted the new commander in chief. Bush returned the salute. The visual storyline was not the "changing of the guard" but the guarding of the change wrought by Reagan's eight years in office.

Widespread Voter Disinterest in 1988

The 1988 downturn in voter interest was spread broadly across the country. Forty-five states and the District of Columbia had a lower voter-turnout rate in 1988 than 1984; Colorado remained the same, while only Massachusetts, New Hampshire, Nebraska, and Nevada posted increases. *(See map, "Where They Voted . . . and Where They Didn't," in the appendix, p. 127.)*

Many reasons for the low voter turnout were offered. As an indicator of voter apathy and cynicism, it might be somewhat overrated, according to one school of thought. For one thing, said Richard Scammon, former director of the U.S. Bureau of the Census: "Peace and prosperity can generally operate to keep the vote down as well as to help the incumbent. In a sense, a low voter turnout is consent. A pool of disinterest may be valuable for a democracy."

Campaigns that once thrived at the grass-roots level—with storefront political headquarters manned by volunteers and stocked with buttons and bumper stickers—are now waged through the more impersonal medium of television. And according to Democratic consultant Mark Mellman, public cynicism about the political process is growing. "There's a sense that the political system is out of their control on one hand and not responsive on the other," Mellman said.

The public's negative reaction was pinpointed in a *New York Times*/CBS News Poll in late October. It indicated that nearly two-thirds of the registered voters were not enamored of either of the major parties' presidential candidates. Slightly more than half of the poll's respondents considered the presidential campaign boring, and nearly half thought that it was more negative than past campaigns.

Many Democrats complained that a more attractive candidate than Michael S. Dukakis could have done a better job in 1988 of activating the various parts of the Democratic coalition, especially blacks. While George Bush defeated Dukakis by 8 percentage points in the nationwide popular vote, he was preferred by a margin twice as large (34-50 percent) in a *New York Times*/CBS News post-election survey of nonvoters.

The survey found nonvoters to be more mobile, less affluent, less educated, less partisan, and less interested in the campaign than those who voted. And they were disproportionately young: 42 percent of all nonvoters, the survey concluded, were under age thirty; roughly 75 percent were under age forty-five.

The 1988 turnout looked much better in terms of the number of registered voters. That number was projected at 130 million by the Committee for the Study of the American Electorate, but because many rolls had not been purged of "deadwood"—people who had not voted in years or even had died since registering—the actual number was believed to be closer to 110 million to 120 million.

If that was a correct assumption, more than three of every four registered voters went to the polls. Nearly 91.6 million Americans actually cast ballots.

Reagan, despite diminished effectiveness in his second term, left office with opinion polls showing his public approval rating higher than 60 percent. The nation even had elevated his vice president to the Oval Office. That had not happened in 152 years, not since Martin Van Buren succeeded Andrew Jackson in 1837. In fact, only two other presidents in this century had the privilege of watching a member of their own party sworn in to succeed them. Both were Republicans, Theodore Roosevelt in 1909 and Calvin Coolidge in 1929.

A 'Kinder, Gentler' Bush

Much of Bush's first days and weeks in office amounted to a get-acquainted period for a nation unaccustomed to new faces in the White House. Reagan had been in the Oval Office longer than anyone since Dwight D. Eisenhower (1953-61). Now, after years in semi-eclipse and a campaign year that featured his fighting side, it was time for the real George Bush to stand up.

Bush now sought a new image—"kinder, gentler" —words from his nomination acceptance speech, echoed in his inaugural address, and repeated endlessly elsewhere. Even at the inauguration, there were reminders of the recent electoral combat—a presidential campaign that was remembered chiefly for its negative character and scarcity of debate on substantive issues. A special train had brought police units to the inaugural festivities from Boston and Springfield, Massachusetts—Michael S. Dukakis's home state. Inauguration officials acknowledged the police were being thanked for their endorsement of Bush, which was used to underscore his attack on Dukakis as a governor "soft on crime."

In the book *The Elections of 1988*, political scientists Francis E. Rourke and John T. Tierney said that from the outset "Bush's strategists recognized that their candidate drew a highly negative rating from voters, while Dukakis was viewed quite favorably. Their solution to this problem was to attack the Democrat's competence and character, a strategy that succeeded perhaps beyond their wildest dreams."

Once victory was in hand, Bush turned to the themes of reconciliation. He was now a good-guy-grandfather with the awkward, spontaneous grin. He spoke of yearning for "an easy-goingness about each other's attitudes and way of life." He was also the new national leader, of course, but he remained reticent about how he planned to run the government. He dampened expectations of major domestic proposals and said he would go slow on foreign initiatives. He mentioned balancing the budget, "hard choices" and "looking at what we have and perhaps allocating it differently. . . ." But he seemed more interested in taking his time than in taking the country by storm. "Some see leadership as high drama, and the sound of trumpets calling," he said. "But I see history as a book with many pages and each day we fill a page with acts of hopefulness and meaning."

The new president offered olive branches all around—to blacks, the young, movement conservatives, hereditary Democrats and, of course, the Congress. In his inaugural speech he called for cooperation with—and from—Speaker Jim Wright, D-Texas, (who waved in response) and Senate Majority Leader George J. Mitchell, D-Maine, (who smiled).

Bush began his first week in office with a pointed, moving appeal to blacks in a speech honoring the Rev. Dr. Martin Luther King, Jr., the late civil rights leader. And in Bush's inaugural address, he had returned to "the homeless, lost and roaming . . . children who have nothing, no love and no normalcy . . . those who cannot free themselves of enslavement to whatever addiction—drugs, welfare, the demoralization that rules the slums." Bush promised no

The People's Choice?

Most presidential winners have sought to portray their victory as a mandate from the American people. But even landslide victors in the nationwide popular vote have been the choice of barely one-third of the entire voting-age population.

The chart below compares the percentage of the popular vote that presidential winners since 1932 have received with the percentage of the entire voting-age population that their vote total represents. The latter percentage is based on voting-age population estimates updated each election year by the Census Bureau.

Year—Winner (Party)	Percentage of Total Popular Vote	Percentage of Voting-Age Population
1932—Roosevelt (D)	57.4	30.1
1936—Roosevelt (D)	60.8	34.6
1940—Roosevelt (D)	54.7	32.2
1944—Roosevelt (D)	53.4	29.9
1948—Truman (D)	49.6	25.3
1952—Eisenhower (R)	55.1	34.0
1956—Eisenhower (R)	57.4	34.1
1960—Kennedy (D)	49.7	31.2
1964—Johnson (D)	61.1	37.8
1968—Nixon (R)	43.4	26.4
1972—Nixon (R)	60.7	33.5
1976—Carter (D)	50.1	26.8
1980—Reagan (R)	50.7	26.7
1984—Reagan (R)	58.8	31.2
1988—Bush (R)	53.4	26.8

new public funds to redress the nation's social ills. Instead he sought an extension of private charity—a concept expressed in his campaign phrase, "a thousand points of light." "We have more will than wallet," he said, "but will is what we need."

"Bush is making the right moves," said Sen. Thomas A. Daschle, D-S.D., co-chairman of the Democratic Policy Committee. The public agreed, according to a *Washington Post*-ABC News poll taken late in March 1989. It indicated that 71 percent of the people approved of the way the president was handling his job. As for Bush's harmony with Congress, Daschle said, it would last until "the first real legislative confrontation comes."

That came soon. For the first time in the Senate's two-hundred-year history, it rejected the cabinet choice of a president beginning his first term. The Senate refused to confirm Bush's nomination of former senator John Tower to be secretary of defense on a 47-53 vote that hewed close to party lines. And yet, both Bush and the leader of the fight against Tower, Sen. Sam Nunn, D-Ga., claimed not to view the vote as a partisan exercise of power.

Bipartisanship Quest

Bush's turn-the-other-cheek reaction to the Tower defeat made clearer that he was depending heavily on developing good relations with Congress. Instead of confronting a balky Congress head-on in the Reagan manner, he would offer compromise. Bush and his budget director, Richard G. Darman, had already sent Congress sketchy budget proposals for fiscal year 1990. The proposals required a large measure of negotiation with Congress as to where much domestic spending would be cut to meet budget-reduction goals that had been written into law.

Although the enactment of a budget necessarily involves the legislative branch, Bush invited Congress to participate in a stage of budget making that previously had been solely an executive function. Some commentators said Bush was cleverly seeking to let Democrats shoulder the blame for unpopular budget cuts, while others said he was engaging in an act of power sharing what would weaken the institution of the presidency.

As an exercise in power sharing, the budget question was soon eclipsed by the implications of an agreement on U.S. policy in Central America. Capping four weeks of intense negotiations led by Secretary of State James A. Baker III, Bush and the top leaders of both parties in Congress signed an accord March 24, 1989, on contra aid, apparently burying a long and contentious issue. It amounted to an abandonment of Reagan's policy of keeping the Nicaraguan guerrillas (contras) armed.

Contra aid would be limited to the non-military kind, as leading Democrats wanted, but could continue until Nicaragua held elections, promised in February 1990, as Bush wanted. In return for the aid extension, Bush promised his full support for diplomatic efforts by Central America's five presidents to end the region's internal wars.

For the first time in years, Bush said, the president and the leaders of both congressional parties were "speaking with one voice about Central America." It gave him a political boost in the wake of widespread complaints in Washington that he had yet to seize the initiative in any area of foreign policy. On the other hand, it created a dispute in the White House—and elsewhere—over whether Congress was constitutionally entitled to share in such a sphere of foreign policy making. The White House counsel, C. Boyden Gray, objected, arguing that Bush was yielding presidential power to Congress. White House Chief of Staff John H. Sununu rebuked Gray for publicly criticizing the accord in a March 26 *New York Times* interview. On an ABC News television show, Baker defended the pact as "a restoration of presidential power."

While the president cultivated the support of Democrats to pass legislation with his imprint, many House Republicans signaled that they were marching to a different drummer. On March 22, 1989, by an 87-85 vote, members of the House Republican Conference elected a strong partisan, Rep. Newt Gingrich of Georgia, over moderate Rep. Edward R. Madigan of Illinois as the chamber's GOP whip—the No. 2 leadership post. It was vacated by Rep. Dick Cheney of Wyoming when Bush appointed him secretary of defense upon Tower's defeat.

Gingrich's drive to define a party message and emphasize differences with Democrats seemed to run counter to Bush's aims of achieving bipartisanship. Gingrich, an outspoken conservative, had earned the enmity of many Democratic leadership loyalists because he had instigated a House ethics committee investigation of Speaker Jim Wright. That inquiry led the panel, formally the Committee on Standards and Official Conduct, to issue a report April 17 accusing Wright of sixty-nine violations of House rules. In its main findings, the twelve-member committee of Democrats and Republicans found "reason to believe" that Wright schemed to evade House limits on non-congressional income and improperly received $145,000 in gifts during the previous decade.

Before the 101st Congress convened, the Senate installed a new set of Democratic leaders, headed by George Mitchell. He replaced Robert C. Byrd, W. Va., who was elected president pro tempore of the Senate, a largely ceremonial office traditionally held by the senior member of the majority party. Wright, who remained as Speaker, opened the 1989 House session with a conciliatory gesture to Republicans, who com-

plained that Democrats had long steamrollered the rights of the minority party. Conceding the need for greater consultation between the parties, Wright said, "The minority has an important and constructive role to play in the legislative process, and I am eager to encourage that role." But familiar party lines immediately were redrawn when Republicans tried to block approval of minor changes in House rules. They lost on a party-line vote.

Quite aside from the added partisanship that likely was injected by the Tower and Wright issues, the new 101st Congress could not be expected to give Bush any room for error. "The country voted for a Democratic legislative branch," House Majority Whip Tony Coelho, D-Calif., boasted on the morning after the election. "We're going to exercise that check on the executive," he insisted. Reagan had entered office with a Republican majority in the Senate and a "working majority" of Republicans and "boll weevil" Democrats in the House; Bush had neither.

2

Losing Power to Congress

When Ronald Reagan handed over the office to his vice president, George Bush, in January 1989, the departing president was as popular as when he came in. As both supporters and critics agreed, Reagan had returned glamour and stature to the office. Nevertheless, a number of White House-watchers said the presidency was far less powerful than Reagan had made it appear during his eight years in office. In that time, it accrued little real authority in terms of the two-hundred-year struggle between the executive and legislative branches of government.

"Despite a tremendous effort to rewrite the theory of the presidency, Reagan leaves no major institutional legacy," said Theodore Lowi, a Cornell University presidential scholar. He did not break through the "institutional barriers," added Stuart E. Eizenstat, who was President Carter's domestic affairs adviser. "Reagan showed that a person with a good mandate, good speaking skills, and a targeted agenda can make the system work," observed Louis Fisher, a constitutional scholar at the Congressional Research Service. "The odd thing is, after the first year, he showed little leadership other than negative."

After eight years in power, hardly any agencies or programs were dismantled. Reagan could not get Congress to approve his social agenda, which featured constitutional amendments to ban abortion and allow school prayer. He attacked Congress for the budget deficits and won the early rounds, but Congress reasserted itself and forced him to embrace the Gramm-Rudman deficit-reduction law, bringing to a halt his great increases in military spending. In foreign policy and war powers, a central motif of Reaganism was that of the strong president acting decisively on the world scene, unencumbered by fussy legislators. Yet the foreign policy successes of the era took place when Reagan's goals meshed with those of Congress. Where Reagan challenged Congress, he often stumbled.

A Weakened Presidency?

It could be said that President Bush inherited as little institutional authority as Reagan himself did from a beleaguered Jimmy Carter in 1981. And lacking Reagan's clear electoral mandate for change, Bush was left with a further paradox: an undertow of constitutional power continued to flow away from the White House toward Congress, while the presidential luster of the Reagan years increased the public's expectation of the chief executive's ability to take command.

Reagan himself recognized the situa-

The Continuing War Powers Debate

Almost from the start, Congress and the Reagan White House squared off repeatedly over foreign policy. The root of nearly every dispute was Reagan's use of military muscle to address foreign policy questions and whether Reagan had the right to use it on his own initiative.

The 1983 invasion of Grenada and the 1986 bomb strike against Libya won broad congressional approval and demonstrated the president's continued flexibility in the case of quick strikes that had little long-term implication for U.S. military involvement.

But on more extended ventures—particularly where the goals seemed unclear or where the threat to the United States was not easy to portray—Congress insisted on involving itself in ways that often set limits on executive action. The question of congressional ability to limit the president's war powers arose in two significant cases: Lebanon and the Persian Gulf.

The Israeli invasion of Lebanon in June 1982 had brought President Reagan into the maelstrom of Middle East politics. At first, Congress offered no resistance to Reagan's order stationing 1,200 Marines in a peacekeeping force in war-torn Beirut. But in September 1983, after the first American troops were killed in combat in Lebanon, Congress gave its reluctant approval to keeping the Marines there for another eighteen months. But in approving that action, Congress for the first time invoked a central provision of the 1973 War Powers Resolution, which requires presidents to withdraw U.S. forces from foreign conflicts within ninety days, absent congressional approval.

No president had ever acknowledged the constitutionality of the War Powers Resolution. Reagan denied its applicability even while signing the new resolution on Lebanon. But in signing it Reagan gave the 1973 act more political validity than it had acquired during its first ten years of existence.

The second case, the president's decision in 1987 to provide U.S. Navy escorts for Kuwaiti oil tankers in the Persian Gulf, provoked a still-unresolved confrontation. Both the House and Senate cast largely symbolic votes in 1987 in favor of delaying deployment of the U.S. ships. The legislative intervention was spawned by the lawmakers' unhappiness that Reagan was committing U.S. forces to a risky mission with no significant congressional consultation.

The issue led to efforts by Senate leaders to revise the War Powers Resolution to give it more force. But there was not enough opposition to the escort policy in the Senate to support a change, and the war powers issue was left hanging. Some observers believed it might be in Bush's long-term interests to support some form of compromise that recognizes his right to take immediate action, subject to informal consultation with congressional leaders. "I think Congress will be receptive to a quid pro quo," said Stuart E. Eizenstat. "The War Powers act has become inappropriate and unworkable. I think it will be changed [in 1989]."

tion. "When I entered office, I found the presidency a weakened institution. I found a Congress that was trying to transform our government into a quasi-parliamentary system," he told his political appointees in a farewell. "I've used the president's ability to frame the broadest outlines of debate to compensate for some of the weakening of the office. But we have not restored the constitutional balance, at least not fully—and I believe it must be restored."

Perhaps no president, no matter how personally popular and skillful, can be persuasive with legislators indefinitely. But Reagan, who never cared much for the folkways of Capitol Hill, was seen as increasingly disengaged. In 1981 Reagan's personal courtship of GOP loyalists helped win a narrow Senate vote approving the sale of advanced radar-equipped aircraft to Saudi Arabia. Late in 1985 he could still go to Congress and persuade House Republicans to vote for tax reform. But it was his last hurrah. In 1987 Reagan vetoed the first two big bills of the year—water treatment and highway construction. Congress promptly overrode both. And when he went to the Capitol to meet with Republican senators voting to override, not one would switch.

Dwight D. Eisenhower, Lyndon B. Johnson, Richard Nixon, Gerald R. Ford, and Carter all shared Reagan's fate of accomplishing less and less legislatively the longer they stayed in office. The decline was sometimes interrupted but never reversed, according to *Congressional Quarterly* analyses of Capitol Hill voting since 1953. The easier trophies were won in the first and second years. After that the fights got tougher. The bloom was off the Rose Garden visits for congressional leaders and committee chairmen. President John F. Kennedy was the lone exception to this trend. He enjoyed more success each year he served, but his time in office—shortened by an assassin—ran to less than three years.

Whenever a Democratic Congress has encountered a new Republican president, the honeymoon has tended to be short and grudging. The most notable periods of cooperation have occurred when a new president's coattails were long enough to bring large numbers of his party's congressional candidates into office. That was Reagan's good fortune but not Bush's. When Reagan won the presidency in 1980, Republicans gained thirty-three House seats and took control of the Senate for the first time in a quarter-century. In the Bush election eight years later, the Democrats gained four seats in the House and one in the Senate, giving them majorities of 260-175 and 55-45 in the two chambers.

Bush's election presented Congress with a new partner but no new set of marching orders. However, in his favor, moderates of both parties in Congress sensed relief from an era of ideological confrontation.

Bush's Stint in Congress

Congress tended to prefer a commitment toward working things out, and so did Bush. Upon entering office, he had shown an aptitude for doing business with Congress, and he had the best credential any new president can have with its members—he was once one of them. Rep. Bill McCollum, R-Fla., said: "He still remembers what it was like."

And yet, in his autobiographical book *Looking Forward,* Bush touched only lightly on his four years as a member of the Republican minority in the House. He recounts those years (1967 through 1970) in fewer than ten pages.

Announcing his first bid for president in 1979, Bush referred to his House service with an ironic joke, implying it had been too brief to be a liability. But if his House seat was far from a career highlight, it was his first public office and arguably the pivotal job on his long résumé of government service.

Before winning the seat in 1966, Bush had been a local businessman, a local party official, and an unsuccessful Senate candidate. After leaving the House, he was continually a national figure—picked for top-level jobs by the president or running for president himself. It was in Congress that Bush had begun building a network of contacts.

He compiled a record that could be presented as either conservative or moderate, depending on one's purpose. Above all, he was a pragmatist, more attuned to the interpersonal dynamics of politics than devoted to ideology—less partisan than the Bush of the 1988 presidential campaign.

Bush's voting was in line with the conservative coalition of Republicans and southern Democrats 83 percent of the time in the 90th Congress but only 60 percent in the 91st, according to *Congressional Quarterly*. The latter score was lowered by Bush's absences in 1970, when his bid for the Senate caused him to miss about two of every five roll call votes. Americans for Democratic Action (ADA), the premier liberal rating group, gave Bush an average rating of just 6.5 percent for the four years he served in the House. The AFL-CIO rated him at an average of 8 percent.

Voting measurements aside, Bush's aura of centrist politics has endured, largely by virtue of his personal contacts and positioning. Bush underlined this impression by being buddies with many Democrats. One was G. V. "Sonny" Montgomery of Mississippi, a southern conservative. But another frequent gym partner from across the aisle was the liberal George E. Brown, Jr., of California.

Those who know Bush well have said that despite the disadvantage of having to deal with a Democratic-controlled Congress, he has had the government experience and temperament to get along well

with the Washington establishment. "I think you'll see pictures of him playing horseshoes with members of Congress," said fellow Texan Robert S. Strauss, a veteran Democratic insider. Democratic leaders have insisted they want to work closely with Bush, if only to avoid a negative backlash from the public. "If we are perceived as obstructionist, or if we are perceived as unwilling to cooperate with the president, we have problems," said Tony Coelho, the House majority whip.

Lawmakers' Partisan Trend

Unfortunately for a president lacking a congressional majority, the trend in Congress has been toward partisanship for the past decade, according to measurements of party unity that *Congressional Quarterly* applied to the lawmakers' voting records. "My antennae ... indicate to me, at least, that the emotional level of partisanship, never mind the voting scores, has risen perceptibly in the last several years" and will continue to do so, said Walter Kravitz, an adjunct professor of political science at Catholic University in Washington, D.C.

The trend suggested that partisanship was likely to be high in Congress during 1989. Since 1970, party unity voting had risen in all but one post-election year. The exception was 1981, when many conservative Democrats deserted their party to support President Reagan's first-year economic agenda.

The reasons for partisan voting trends were not always clear. In recent years, voting patterns had shown a drop in support for the president and a diminished role for the coalition of Republicans and conservative southern Democrats that was very visible in 1981. One explanation was that when fewer Democrats supported a Republican president, the odds were better that majorities of the two parties would oppose each other.

In large part, the coalition's poor showing in recent years could be chalked up to a lack of ideological issues that divide the parties along liberal-conservative lines. But the coalition's decline also could be attributed to more subtle and enduring reasons. In 1981 Reagan swept into office with a tax- and budget-cutting agenda that few Republicans and southern Democrats could resist. But after that, said Rep. Dave McCurdy, D-Okla., "Ronald Reagan lost his agenda," depriving conservatives of a leader.

"Democrats trying to limit the impact of the Reagan agenda ... [were] particularly noticeable after the 1982 election, and it strengthened the partisan trend in Congress," said Patricia Hurley, a political science professor at Texas A&M University. The selection of Jim Wright as House Speaker in 1987 was perceived on both sides of the aisle as stimulating partisanship in that chamber.

But the battles between Reagan and Congress did not fully explain the trend. After all, partisanship was growing when Carter was in the White House. Nor did it appear that the election of George Bush—a man who wanted to negotiate with Congress—would guarantee less partisanship.

3

The Deficit Dilemma

Because the federal deficit dominated and defined so much of the national agenda when the Bush administration took office, it was necessarily a source of partisan division. Nevertheless, the political choices required for a balanced budget were so difficult that almost everyone from Capitol Hill to the White House had an incentive to stall—unless the country suffered a crisis more severe than the October 1987 stock market crash.

In this political atmosphere, the Gramm-Rudman law requiring a balanced budget by 1993 was ripe for further change or circumvention. As originally enacted in 1985, the law required a balanced budget by fiscal 1991. In 1987, Congress acknowledged this aim was impossible by extending the deadline two years.

The law is formally titled the Balanced Budget and Emergency Deficit Control Act, but is generally known as Gramm-Rudman, a name derived from two of its three principal architects: Sen. Phil Gramm, R-Texas, Sen. Warren B. Rudman, R-N.H., and Sen. Ernest F. Hollings, D-S.C. They and like-minded colleagues turned to that device out of frustration over the unwillingness of the White House and Congress to use existing controls to break a deficit-spending habit then running at $150-$200 billion a year.

The government has not had a balanced budget since 1969, but until the Reagan years the deficits were of a lower order. During his eight years in office, Reagan saw the national debt more than doubled, breaking the $2 trillion mark. As a result, the government has been forced to borrow increasingly larger amounts of money, mainly through the sale of notes, bonds, and other government securities.

Hanging overhead was President Bush's campaign pledge never to raise taxes or cut Social Security benefits. The promises may be as difficult to keep as the legal commitment to balance the budget. During the election campaign, Bush vaguely sketched out a "flexible freeze" plan, which he said would allow defense spending and domestic entitlement programs to grow with inflation, while extracting some cuts from unspecified spending accounts. The plan for "growing out of the deficit" relies heavily on the continuation of at least 3 percent real growth in the economy for the next five years to generate revenues, and on an immediate 2 percent reduction in short-term interest rates to save costs. Many economic experts viewed these expectations as unrealistic. Interest rates started an upward climb in 1988 that carried over into 1989. To sustain 3 percent growth after inflation for five years was a tall order for the healthiest of economies.

The difficulty for Bush—and for his Democratic foes in Congress—began with a fundamental question: What was an acceptable deficit? How each side chose to answer that question would frame much of the debate over budget issues throughout Bush's term in office. Many economists believed a balanced budget was a misleading or meaningless way to measure the government's fiscal soundness. In some years a big deficit might reflect only a temporary situation, such as when the nation goes to war or responds to unpredictable natural disasters. Other times the deficit, because of the complicated way it is calculated, does not reveal true shortfalls in government accounts.

The surplus in the Social Security trust funds, for example, made the shortfall in the rest of the federal budget look smaller than it would otherwise appear. Yet there were important reasons for combining the figures into a single calculation of the government's effect on the economy. Indeed, whether the government's annual deficit was reported at $10 billion, $100 billion, or $200 billion often mattered less than its size compared with the rest of the economy.

The $155 billion deficit recorded in fiscal 1988 equaled 3.2 percent of the nation's gross national product (GNP), the standard measure of the economy's size and annual growth. While still large compared with those of previous administrations, that deficit-GNP ratio was well below that of Reagan's first full year in office, when a smaller deficit of $128 billion represented 4.1 percent of the GNP.

Even in percentage terms, however, the Reagan-era deficits have been monumental. The deficit claimed as much as 6.3 percent of GNP in fiscal 1983 (when the government's shortfall topped $200 billion for the first time), and it averaged 4.7 percent during Reagan's first seven years in office. From the end of World War II until Reagan entered the Oval Office, the average deficit-GNP ratio was 1.8 percent. From the close of the Vietnam War through Jimmy Carter's presidency, the main fear of budget makers was that continued deficits would overheat the economy and result in runaway inflation.

It was in such a period of unbridled inflation and stagnated economic growth—stagflation—that Reagan came to power. His promise to cut taxes, balance the budget, and bring the national debt under control was a rallying cry for those who believed that irresponsible fiscal policy—that is, too much government spending—had ruined the economy. Reagan fulfilled his promise to cut taxes, but he never managed to bring down federal spending. Surprisingly, the Federal Reserve Board, chaired by Paul Volcker, managed to bring inflation under control even while federal deficits leaped to once-unthinkable heights. In 1986, the year the annual deficit reached its all-time record of $221.2 billion, the Consumer Price Index actually fell from 3.6 percent to 1.9 percent.

Do Deficits Matter?

"There is no level of deficit that in and of itself is seen as a disaster," said Norman J. Ornstein, a student of Congress at the American Enterprise Institute. Budget makers no longer could know what level of deficit spending was acceptable. In the 1970s, most experts believed a $100 billion deficit would wreck the economy. Instead, the economy thrived while the government experienced deficits twice that size.

Two leading conservative economists who were Bush's campaign advisers—Michael Boskin of Stanford University, who became chairman of the new president's Council of Economic Advisers, and Richard Rahn of the U.S. Chamber of Commerce—have insisted that the current deficit level should be no cause for alarm. They saw the

Gramm-Rudman: Who Benefits?

In passing the Gramm-Rudman deficit-reduction act, Congress effectively limited its spending prerogatives with a novel provision. Automatic, across-the-board cuts would be ordered if deficit-reduction targets were not met. Half the cuts were to come from defense, half from selected domestic programs.

In 1986 the Supreme Court struck down the original Gramm-Rudman law, which assigned responsibility for determining the size of the budget cuts and for executing the automatic cuts to the General Accounting Office, a legislative arm. As the 1985 law was amended in 1987, the president's budget director was given sole authority to calculate the economic projections that would determine the size of the automatic cuts. Some Republican strategists believed the president regained power over the budget process. "It takes spending power away from Congress," said Stephen Bell, former Senate Budget Committee staff director, adding: "Anything that diminishes the power of Congress enhances the power of the president."

But budget scholar Allen Schick of the University of Maryland said the side that most feared the Gramm-Rudman cuts was automatically put in a weaker bargaining position. When Democrats wanted to avoid cuts in social programs, President Reagan gained leverage in budget negotiations. It has since appeared, however, that the deepest worries have shifted to the White House and Pentagon, since the most politically sensitive domestic programs have been exempted.

"There is nothing inherent in Gramm-Rudman that tilts it to the advantage of one branch," Schick said. "It only tilts when one side says that [cuts] are unacceptable. If Bush believes that, then he has to deal with Congress on its terms."

1988 deficit-GNP ratio as evidence that the growing economy would take care of the shortfall; the 1988 deficit was 3.2 percent of GNP, down from its peak of 6.3 percent five years earlier.

"A tax increase would slow economic growth," Rahn maintained. "Its effect on reducing the deficit will be minuscule, but its effect on the economy may be devastating." Even some politically liberal economists have begun to share the idea that the nation can "grow out of the deficit," while others have been urging lawmakers not to overreact with quick fixes to balance the budget. In contrast, Peter G. Peterson, for-

mer secretary of commerce under President Richard Nixon and chairman of the Blackstone Group, an investment consulting firm, held the view that the nation must undergo a long period of hard sacrifice to bring down the national debt and ensure prosperity for the future.

Robert Reischauer, a Brookings Institution scholar who advised Democrat Michael S. Dukakis's presidential campaign, agreed. He voiced a widely held belief that future economic growth hinges on the nation's ability to invest in the future. But because of federal deficits, the government uses up much of its investment capital to finance its debt. As a result, the U.S. economy has had to rely more and more on foreign investments. But even the economists who believed that deficits were still a danger to the U.S. economy conceded that the real consequences would not appear until long into the future.

To increase living standards for the next generation, however, would require eliminating the deficit, not just reducing it, insisted Brookings economist Alice M. Rivlin, former director of the Congressional Budget Office. "The real question is, can you sell it to the president?" said Rivlin. "We've got eight years of history to prove that Congress, if it has to fight the president, doesn't solve the deficit by itself. It takes executive leadership," she said.

While economic questions underlay the debate on the deficit, the issue would in fact be fought out in political terms. "It's entirely political," said Stanley E. Collender, author of *The Guide to the Federal Budget.* "And politically, it will never be possible to say a balanced budget is not necessary." The call for a balanced budget has been a dividing issue for two fundamental visions of government and society since the early days of the republic, historian James D. Savage has observed in *Balanced Budgets and American Politics.*

Alexander Hamilton took a sanguine view of deficits and debt, revealing his Federalist passion for a strong central government. "A national debt if it is not excessive will be to us a national blessing; it will be a powerful cement of our union," Hamilton stated in 1781. Hamilton and his disciples lost that argument to Thomas Jefferson, Andrew Jackson, and other early Democrats who believed a balanced national budget symbolized the dream of an agrarian, states-oriented government. It reflected their populist desire "to limit the purpose and size of the federal government, to restrain its influence in the economy, and to promote republican virtue," Savage wrote.

Deficit spending was not politically tolerated until the 1930s, when Franklin D. Roosevelt reinvigorated a depression economy with federal dollars. Only after Roosevelt launched the New Deal did British economist John Maynard Keynes lay out a theory of how increased government spending could reduce unemployment and stimulate the entire economy. "Keynes provided a sophisticated rationale for what Roosevelt was doing anyway," said Herbert Stein, a conservative economist.

The Keynesian theory underlay deficit-spending fiscal policies of John F. Kennedy, Lyndon B. Johnson, and even Nixon. "I am now a Keynesian," Nixon said in defense of his budgetary response to the 1970 recession. But as the Vietnam War accelerated deficit spending, the government's ability to control the economy through fiscal policy became increasingly limited. By the end of Gerald R. Ford's administration, deficit spending was once again transformed into a symbol of inefficient and wasteful government. Carter, for one, traded on that idea. He came to Washington saying that deficits were the source of the nation's economic and social "malaise," although he too was unable to balance the budget.

Reagan entered office with a fiscal policy based on "supply-side" economics. Diametrically opposed to Keynesian ideas about the power of government spending, the supply-siders insisted the economy would rebound only when tax rates were cut, giving consumers and corporations more money to spend. Thus Reagan placed himself squarely in the populist tradition of Thomas Jefferson and Andrew Jackson, who fought for a lean federal government and greater economic leeway for individuals. In the process, however, Reagan and the Republican party were caught in a cruel economic irony.

Though he managed to cut taxes, Reagan could not sufficiently rein in spending. The economy rebounded in the 1980s, but at the same time Reagan had saddled the country with huge debts. As a result, Republicans were forced to minimize the significance of deficit spending and Democrats became its critics. "I see the rhetoric going that way," Savage said in an interview. "But it's very shortsighted. If you are a Democrat and believe you should have an activist fiscal policy, you don't want to say you have to have a balanced budget. It takes a tool out of your hands."

Bush's Inheritance

George Bush came into office against this backdrop of conflicting economic theories and shifting trends. He brought with him a goal to cut spending, a pledge to resist any new taxes, and a pressing need—in the view of some veteran budget practitioners—to get around the immediate budgetary restrictions of the Gramm-Rudman law.

"Bush is banking on Democrats to drag him kicking and screaming to new taxes," said a Republican member of Congress. But Democratic strategists showed no intention of taking the first step, as House Majority Leader Jim Wright did in early 1986 with his call for new taxes. Bush made such an issue of opposing any form of tax hike that Democrats intend to make him eat his words.

As it had since 1985, Gramm-Rudman would set the boundaries of debate as well as the timing of all decision making on the budget. The law set a deficit ceiling of $100 billion for fiscal 1990, and it required automatic cutbacks in defense and domestic programs if Congress and the president could not agree on sufficient savings by September 15, 1989. Bush calculated that the budget proposals he sent to Congress on February 9 would require $1.16 trillion in fiscal 1990 spending. That figure fell $94.8 billion short of estimated revenues but within the limits of Gramm-Rudman. How-

ever, his budget—a revision of the one Reagan had sent to Congress shortly before leaving office—offered few details and included $16 billion in unspecified cuts—$9 billion of them in defense, $5 billion in Medicare, and $2 billion in agriculture. He called on Pentagon officials to recommend within sixty days where to apply the defense cuts.

And while Bush requested a number of increases for specific space and science programs, environmental-protection efforts, homeless-aid initiatives, and nuclear-weapons-plant cleanup, among others, he offered only a lump sum of $136 billion to cover all other domestic programs that are funded through annual appropriations. Since that was the same amount those programs were financed in 1989, it meant that some programs would have to be cut back or eliminated for others to keep pace with inflation. The president suggested some trade-offs—cutting Amtrak and mass-transit subsidies in exchange for nutrition and welfare increases, for example. But otherwise he remained silent on some eighty programs that Reagan wanted to eliminate.

It was an approach that allowed Bush to outline programs and priorities he wanted to emphasize or add, and yet distance himself from the tightfisted image of his predecessor. In an address to Congress on his budget proposals, Bush said that "we must establish some very clear priorities, and we must make a very substantial cut in the federal budget deficit." He then invited Congress to negotiate the solutions with him.

Congressional Democrats, while responding positively to the conciliatory tone of Bush's speech, were quick to point out what they viewed as the shortcomings of his budget proposals. "It's not really a budget," said Jim Sasser, D-Tenn., chairman of the Senate Budget Committee.

Despite complaints from Democrats that they had been handed the unwanted job of cutting popular programs, House and Senate budget committee leaders soon began meeting with White House officials to conduct budget "negotiations." On April 14, 1989, a bipartisan contingent of House and Senate leaders gathered in the White House Rose Garden to announce an "agreement" to cut $28 billion from the fiscal 1990 budget.

They revealed a skeletal package of reductions, about equally divided between broad spending cuts and yet-to-be determined revenue increases, intended to bring the deficit slightly below the Gramm-Rudman ceiling of $100 billion. But the agreement did little more than chart a fleeting escape from seemingly intractable contradictions in U.S. fiscal policy.

A chunk of the $13.8 billion in proposed spending cuts involved one-time windfalls or other accounting gimmicks that would not carry over into future years. More important, the deal was based on the administration's rosy assumptions of national economic growth to produce the bulk of the projected $14.7 billion in new revenues.

One issue the budget makers have had to struggle with was how much the government could afford to spend to rescue bankrupt savings and loan institutions. Heavy initial outlays would presumably lessen the total bill over the long haul, but would drive the budget up through the deficit limits.

4

Bailouts for S&Ls and Foreign Debtors

Waiting at the doorstep of 1600 Pennsylvania Avenue on January 20 was the savings and loan industry, hat in hand. The government closed or sold off more than two hundred bankrupt savings and loan institutions in 1988, half of them in the last three months of the year. Many more were insolvent but remained open only because the federally guaranteed insurance fund was depleted and the depositors could not be paid off. The Federal Home Loan Bank Board reported that losses among the nation's three thousand federally insured savings and loans ("S&Ls") or "thrifts" amounted to $7.8 billion in 1987 and $12.1 billion in 1988.

To replenish the insurance fund might eventually cost taxpayers $100 billion or more, according to many estimates. But with tens of thousands of depositors facing the loss of their savings, and all the thrifts in danger of losing the public's confidence, the government had to act.

Since neither the White House nor Congress had any desire to tackle the issue head-on in a presidential election year, the postponed S&L crisis immediately became a priority concern for the new president. Even before George Bush entered the Oval Office, Treasury officials and pertinent regulatory agencies were put to work hammering out a bailout plan, which Bush unveiled

in broad outline on February 6, 1989. It called for selling the remaining bankrupt savings institutions to investors during the next five years or simply closing them down and paying off the depositors from an insurance fund that would be fed through a complex set of long-term financial arrangements. The cost would be borne by both the taxpayers and the two thousand or so still-healthy savings institutions.

Thrift-industry spokesmen, who two years earlier were saying there was no need for an extensive bailout, had meanwhile changed their tune. But they thought it was the government's duty, not theirs, to foot the bill. They blamed Congress, federal regulators, and the states for letting some thrift operators get away with questionable or even fraudulent practices. Congress tended to blame the federal regulators for not properly overseeing the industry.

To some degree, this large number of closures amounted to an admission that critics were right: The regulators had moved too slowly to prevent such a calamity. Congress, too, shared in the responsibility. House Speaker Jim Wright, for one, was accused of listening to questionable thrift operators in Texas, his home state. In 1986 he helped scuttle an administration-requested recapitalization for the Federal Savings and Loan Insurance Corporation

(FSLIC), the federal agency that guarantees S&L deposits up to $100,000 each. He argued that the Federal Home Loan Bank Board, which oversees the FSLIC, should go easy on failing thrifts in Texas where a drop in oil prices had created a recession. His role on behalf of the S&Ls became part of a House ethics committee investigation into his dealings.

Bush's S&L Rescue

Although much of Bush's bailout plan required approval by Congress, the administration began putting other parts of it into effect. The FSLIC and the still-solvent Federal Deposit Insurance Corporation (FDIC), a counterpart agency that insures bank deposits, were to be merged and placed under the Treasury Department. The two agencies began to combine their operations February 7, and some savings institutions were already being seized by federal regulators. By early spring, more than five hundred S&Ls were considered insolvent.

Congress received Bush's plan with some skepticism, thinking its cost estimates understated. It projected total bailout spending in excess of $148 billion by the end of the century, of which $60 billion would come from the nation's taxpayers. The total figure was later restated at $156.7 billion, and some estimates of taxpayer assistance over the next three decades ran to more than $100 billion.

Bush proposed to finance the bailout through a sale of bonds that would be repaid over a period of thirty years. Interest on the bonds would be guaranteed by the U.S. Treasury and paid by both the taxpayers and solvent S&Ls through their deposit-insurance premiums. These bonds would be covered by an equivalent amount of bonds that would be purchased at a deep discount by a yet-to-be-created agency. The money to buy the "equivalent" bonds would come from the insurance premiums and from retained earnings of the twelve Federal Home Loan Banks. Those earnings were owed to savings institutions that held stock in the banks.

Through this elaborate arrangement, some $50 billion would become available for bailout purposes during the next three years, according to the plan. Taxpayers would also be asked to pick up $40 billion in promissory notes and other guarantees that the FSLIC gave in lieu of cash to buyers of defunct savings institutions in 1988. Interest costs would drive the figures even higher over the coming decades. Whatever the ultimate bill turned out to be, it already was clear that this would be the costliest bailout of an industry the government had ever undertaken.

M. Danny Wall, the bank board chairman, told Congress that the cost of closing the 205 S&Ls in 1988 would exceed $32 billion. Although that $32 billion was recorded as having been spent, it was virtually all in the form of ten-year notes and long-term guarantees of the book value of questionable loans included in the thrift deals. To cover those notes and guarantees, Wall said, the FSLIC committed nearly all of its anticipated collections from insurance premiums and the returns on its sale of assets seized from failed thrifts. Without new funds, it would soon be impossible to issue new promissory notes or asset guarantees in order to close other ailing savings institutions. The General Accounting Office, an agency of Congress, said that over the next ten years the FSLIC would fall short of covering existing notes and guarantees by $26 billion.

The 'Thrifts' Object

In congressional hearings, the Bush plan came under attack from the savings and loan industry, still a strong lobbying force despite some loss of credibility resulting from its financial troubles. Officials of the industry said its share of the cost burden was excessive. And they objected to a provision of the plan for eliminating the Federal Home Loan Bank Board, thereby transferring its function of chartering savings institutions to the Treasury Department.

The Rev. Jesse L. Jackson, a contender for the Democratic presidential nomination in 1988, joined a host of other community and religious leaders in denouncing the plan as too costly to most citizens. He said the the average family could end up paying an additional $1,000 in taxes over the years. Jackson also criticized the plan because it did not require the savings industry to add to the stock of low- and moderate-income housing. S&Ls traditionally have been the main source of mortgage lending. The idea of requiring the industry to contribute more to housing construction won the general endorsement of both Jack F. Kemp, Bush's secretary of housing and urban development, and Rep. Henry B. Gonzalez, D-Texas, chairman of the House Banking Committee.

Administration officials, including Treasury Secretary Nicholas F. Brady, urged Congress to approve the plan swiftly, for delay would run up the eventual cost. However, Brady argued against committing the government to more than $10 billion in bailout expenditures in fiscal year 1989. Any more, he told a meeting of business executives in Dallas on March 28, would cause the year's budget deficit to rupture the Gramm-Rudman ceiling.

Third World Debt

The threat to the thrift industry was only one of this nation's economic concerns for the incoming Bush administration. Fears of rising inflation and interest rates, and, consequently, the stability of the dollar and Third World debtor nations occupied the thoughts of Washington's economic strategists.

For much of the previous three years, while he was secretary of the treasury, James A. Baker III guided a steady decline of the dollar strength against other leading currencies. The goal was to increase exports by making them cheaper abroad and to reduce imports by making them costlier at home—and thus to reduce or eliminate the U.S. foreign trade deficit. To a large degree that tactic seemed to succeed. Exports rose substantially, and the economy continued to grow. In 1988 the dollar first stabilized and then rebounded slightly, suggesting that its controlled fall was sufficient to restore market confidence. Under Baker's leadership the world's seven largest industrial countries apparently agreed that currency exchange rates should remain fairly stable.

But renewed fears of inflation at home and abroad began boosting interest rates, a worrisome situation for the dollar. The Federal Reserve Board, apparently to stem the U.S. inflationary thrust, took the largely unexpected step in July 1988 of increasing the rate at which it lends to member banks. That led to an immediate boost in the prime rate—a benchmark for commercial and consumer lending—to double digits for the first time in more than three years.

President Ronald Reagan's economic forecasters contended that long- and short-term interest rates would decline in 1989. Congressional forecasters and many private economists disagreed. In the early months of the year, consumer prices were growing at an annual rate of above 5 percent, roughly doubling the pace of two and three years earlier, but far behind the 13.5 percent inflation of 1980 during President Jimmy Carter's last year in office.

Higher interest rates made it far more costly for the government to refinance its $2 trillion debt—initially estimated at $220 billion in fiscal 1989—which accounted for roughly 14 percent of the year's federal spending. From an international perspective, higher interest rates attract foreign investors. The resulting demand for dollars to invest would push their value higher and possibly create instability on international money markets.

If the dollar did not remain stable, there was a danger that the recently improved trade deficit would worsen. Most economists blamed the severity of the nation's recent trade imbalance with the rest of the world on the dollar's precipitous climb in the wake of inflation and higher interest rates in the late 1970s and early 1980s. Recent trade improvements have come only after years of forcing the dollar back down.

Interest rate rises and increases in the value of the dollar also had ominous consequences for Third World economies, and, by extension, for the United States. Almost half of the developing world's $1.1 trillion in foreign debt was owed by seventeen countries, twelve of which were in Latin America and the Caribbean. Those countries, particularly Brazil and Argentina, once were strong markets for U.S.-produced goods. But by 1989, they not only could not buy as much from the United States, they were having trouble making payments on their loans.

Brady's Debt-Relief Plan

While Baker might have scored a success with the dollar, his equally well-known proposals for easing the Third World's debt did not fare so well. He sought to encourage commercial-bank lending to the already heavily indebted countries, especially in Latin America, as a means of stimulating their economies so they could eventually "grow" out of their debts. Yet lending to those countries had fallen; and when principal and interest payments were factored in, they had suffered a net outflow of money.

Large U.S. banks had made some progress in reducing the amount of debt exposure to the Third World. But if rising interest rates prompted a new debt crisis, they could find their situation more precarious. Many administration critics—on and off Capitol Hill—contended that the time was past for a holding action on Third World debt, which was how some characterized Baker's plan. Debt relief for borrowing countries, they said, was essential for economic improvement and must involve some forgiveness, some loan restructuring, and some essential changes in the economies of the borrowing countries.

Nicholas Brady, Baker's successor at Treasury, announced the outline of a plan on March 10, 1989, that encompassed those elements to ease the debt burden of the Third World, especially Latin America. That same day, David C. Mulfor, who had been designated under secretary of the treasury, testified to House and Senate committees that the plan would lead to 20 percent reductions in the overall debts of thirty-nine heavily indebted countries. Officials in the affected countries said they wanted much more debt relief than the plan offered. President Carlos Andres Pérez of Venezuela, for instance, said the Brady plan had raised hopes that the debts might be cut in half.

A key element of the plan was some form of "guarantee"—although Treasury officials shunned the word—of repayment to the commercial banks for their future Third World lending. In return, the banks would write off part of their outstanding loans to the heavily indebted poor countries or sharply reduce the interest requirements.

The guarantee would be backed up by $25 billion from the World Bank and the International Monetary Fund (IMF), which get seed capital from 151 member governments. Part of that amount might be channeled to debtor countries to replenish cash reserves that they used to buy back some of their debt at a discount. The world's leading industrial nations, and the steering committees of the World Bank and IMF, offered only qualified endorsement of Treasury's plan at meetings in Washington in April. The two international lending agencies set up study groups to recommend ways to implement the plan. Soon afterward, the IMF worked out a tentative agreement for the first nation, Mexico, to borrow under the plan's terms. Such borrowing would ease that country's efforts to finance its foreign debt of more than $100 billion.

Since the United States is a major contributor to the World Bank and IMF, it was clear that some U.S. taxpayers' money would be put at risk by the plan. However, many critics of past debt policy argued that some taxpayer money was already placed at risk by the inability of many countries to pay the debts they had already incurred.

5

What Gorbachev's
Soviet Union Portends

For all of the problems that tightened purse strings created for George Bush in his conduct of U.S. foreign relations, there was nevertheless some good news. Disarmament, rather than armament, was at the top of the international agenda. A thaw in U.S.-Soviet relations offered the best chance in more than a decade for moving beyond the cold war. Soviet leader Mikhail S. Gorbachev, suffering financial woes of his own and seeking to rejuvenate his country's political and economic systems, had taken the initiative in challenging the assumption that Washington and Moscow were implacable enemies with a wide range of irreconcilable interests.

In beginning to pull out of costly commitments to expand the Soviet empire, Gorbachev slowly was removing a fundamental issue between the two superpowers. How far he was prepared to go remained to be seen, but the initial evidence pointed to an era of Soviet internal reform rather than outward expansionism. While offering extraordinary opportunities for peace, Gorbachev's bold moves also posed potential risks for the United States and its new president. Just as the Nixon-era détente was clouded by the Soviet buildup of the 1970s, the latest superpower warming trend could

be destroyed by false steps or unrealistic hopes.

Despite five meetings in three years between Gorbachev and Ronald Reagan, and dramatic political changes within the Soviet Union, there were only tentative signs of a fundamental shift in the U.S.-Soviet relationship. Washington and Moscow were treating each other in a more businesslike way, foregoing the harsh rhetoric of the early 1980s. But the two superpowers remained sharply at odds ideologically and held conflicting interests in most corners of the world. Whether the new, more civil tone remained during the Bush presidency would depend partly on political factors in each country.

Gorbachev seemed determined to concentrate on internal economic and political reform, a task that would divert energy away from global adventurism. If his statements could be taken at face value—a big if—they pointed to a new Soviet foreign policy based on the belief that neither superpower could gain permanent superiority through an arms race. In rhetoric, at least, Gorbachev seemed ready to adopt "peaceful coexistence" as a working policy rather than as a cover for expansionism and military buildup.

Aside from the question of whether Gorbachev really meant to apply the policy, Bush had to weigh two other questions: How securely did Gorbachev sit atop the Soviet governing hierarchy? And how deeply into Soviet political life could he embed his new approach to ensure that no successor could easily revert to the old ways? Like Reagan, Bush had to accept that the American public would not tolerate suspension of arms control negotiations as a bargaining tactic against the Soviets.

Disarmament Shifts

When he came to office, Reagan attacked the key arms control accords of the 1970s as too favorable to Moscow. He faulted the 1972 strategic arms limitation treaty (SALT I) and the unratified 1979 SALT II for not cutting the number of strategic nuclear weapons that were deployed. He called for radical cuts: abolition of intermediate-range nuclear-force (INF) missiles in Europe and "deep cuts" in the number of strategic-range missile warheads.

Mainstream specialists in nuclear strategy saw no particular merit in either of these proposals. According to then-prevailing policy of the North Atlantic Treaty Organization (NATO), abolition of the INF missiles would leave the alliance at a disadvantage against the more numerous conventional forces of the Soviet-led Warsaw Pact nations of Eastern Europe. Critics branded Reagan's proposals a ploy—that he offered sweeping reductions Moscow likely would reject as a means of deflecting domestic pressure for arms control.

But Reagan's calls for sweeping cuts seemed also to reflect a deep personal revulsion at the destructiveness of nuclear weapons. He apparently disagreed with orthodox strategic thinkers who regarded the threat of nuclear annihilation as a permanent fixture. In 1983 he called for a strategic defense initiative (SDI) to make nuclear missiles "impotent and obsolete"—a goal that most defense specialists deemed impossible.

By 1985, the year the charismatic Gorbachev came to power, the Kremlin had failed to turn the European members of NATO against deployment of INF missiles. To the astonishment of defense specialists, the Soviet government began moving toward the U.S. disarmament positions. At an October 1986 summit meeting in Iceland, Reagan and Gorbachev discussed the total abolition of nuclear ballistic missiles—and, by some versions of the meeting, of all nuclear weapons. Those proposals were sidetracked by Reagan's refusal to discuss any limits on SDI.

But the next year the two men signed a treaty abolishing INF missiles. And by then they had agreed on the outlines of an arms-reduction deal that would cut roughly in half the number of warheads on strategic ballistic missiles. Only a few conservatives opposed the INF pact. But many other national security specialists from the right and center of the political spectrum—including some prominent Democrats—mobilized to head off further radical cutbacks.

Bush's Position

Since Reagan put his authority as a defense hard-liner behind the notion of halving the number of strategic-missile warheads, it was unlikely that Bush could back away from that general approach. Bush promised to negotiate a cutback in Moscow's conventional forces in Europe before any further major cuts were made in U.S. nuclear weapons. Each of his actions would no doubt be guided as much by domestic politics as by events overseas. The new president likely wanted to appear just as tough and firm as Reagan had.

When Reagan visited the Kremlin in May 1988 and declared that the Soviet empire was no longer "evil," he altered the

American political landscape by undercutting his own political allies who argued that the United States could afford no accommodation with Moscow. The Reaganauts who dominated foreign and defense policy in his first term were saddened and frustrated, not converted, by the change of tone. They remained skeptical of Gorbachev's new, reasonable stance, seeing behind it the same old Soviet state wedded to expansionist policies. They also were concerned that public opinion would find in the new relationship a warrant to abandon the costly U.S. military buildup that—these critics contended—caused the Russians to show more moderation.

Well-placed on Capitol Hill and in GOP-oriented think tanks, the Reaganauts still could exercise a strong influence on policy toward Moscow. Months before his formal designation as the Republican presidential nominee, Bush had distanced himself from some of Reagan's more exuberant declarations that the Russians were turning a corner. Bush probably calmed some of the hard-line critics' fears the month before he entered office. After joining Reagan in a meeting with Gorbachev in New York, Bush stated December 13, 1988, that there was "no way" his administration would be ready to begin detailed strategic arms negotiations with Moscow by the scheduled date of February 15.

"It is a time of great change in the world—and especially in the Soviet Union," Bush said in his first address to Congress on February 9, 1989. "Prudence and common sense dictate that we try to understand the full meaning of the change going on there, review our policies carefully, and proceed with caution," he added. "But I have personally assured General Secretary Gorbachev that, at the conclusion of such a review, we will be ready to move forward. We will not miss an opportunity to work for peace."

Secretary of State James A. Baker III met with Soviet Foreign Minister Eduard A. Shevardnadze in Vienna on March 7 and told reporters he would go to Moscow in May to discuss the resumption of strategic arms negotiations and the possibility of a summit meeting between Bush and Gorbachev. At Vienna, Shevardnadze placed on the negotiating table a proposal to reduce troops and tactical warplanes in Europe over the next three years, leaving the numerical strength of each side 10 to 15 percent below the present NATO levels. Gorbachev, in a December 7, 1988, address to the United Nations General Assembly in New York, had already announced a unilateral reduction of Soviet forces in Europe. The Vienna proposal would cut much deeper into their strength.

Although conventional arms control talks had long been conducted in Vienna, the issue was largely ignored by Western defense specialists until very recently. Thus there was no time-honored U.S. negotiating position. America's allies in Europe would likely insist on a bigger voice than they had had in the nuclear arms talks. British Foreign Secretary Geoffrey Howe said upon hearing Shevardnadze's plan, "Soviet thinking is in many ways close to our own."

Regional Conflicts

Over the years, some of the most difficult bargaining with Moscow concerned distant parts of the world where the superpowers had competing interests. By a remarkable convergence of events, negotiated settlements were reached in three longstanding regional conflicts during 1988. In April, the Soviet Union formally agreed to end its occupation of Afghanistan, which was then in its ninth year and coming under increasingly heavier attack by Afghan guerrillas; within a year of the agreement—involving Moscow, its Soviet-backed Afghan government, Pakistan, and the United States—Soviet troops had pulled out.

That July, Iran and Iraq signed a cease-fire in their eight-year-old war in the Persian Gulf, which at times had inflicted casualties on American warships and sailors whom Reagan had sent to the region to keep the vital waterway open to international shipping. And in December foreign ministers of Angola, Cuba, and South Africa signed a peace accord in a decades-old conflict in southern Africa. The agreement, engineered chiefly by State Department official Chester Crocker, called for the staggered withdrawal of Soviet-backed Cuban troops from Angola and independence for South African-controlled Namibia.

In all three regions, the United States and the Soviet Union found a mutual interest in bringing these hostilities to an end. However, lasting peace was not assured in any of the three regions. And if any of the agreements fell apart, there was no certainty that a U.S.-Soviet rivalry might not be renewed. There had been particular concern that the cease-fire in the Persian Gulf could revitalize the decades-old competition between the United States and the Soviet Union for influence there.

Shevardnadze visited Iran in February 1989 and, as reported in radio broadcasts from Tehran, urged closer ties with the Soviet Union. The same broadcast reported that Ayatollah Ruhollah Khomeini welcomed the offer and urged close cooperation between the two countries to "combat devilish acts in the West." The Iranian leader apparently referred to the British publication of *The Satanic Verses.* The book's unfavorable allusions to the Prophet Mohammed caused outrage in the Islamic world, prompting Khomeini to call on Moslems to kill the author, Salman Rushdie, an Indian-born former Moslem who was living in Britain. The British government broke relations with Iran over the issue. After Iran and Iraq had signed a cease-fire, both Washington and Tehran dropped some clues that each wanted to foster better

relations, but the Rushdie affair appeared to block any further gestures toward reconciliation.

The Kremlin's relations with Moslem countries apparently had improved since its pullout from Afghanistan. Shevardnadze was well received not only in Tehran but in Arab capitals during his tour of the Middle East in February. In Cairo, he made clear that the Soviet Union intended to play an active role in whatever international sponsorship was devised for negotiating an Arab-Israeli peace settlement. In pushing a Middle East peace plan in 1988, the United States welcomed Soviet assistance. That initiative failed, but another was developing in 1989 in an effort to resolve the Palestinian demand for "statehood" in the Israeli-occupied West Bank and Jordan.

Implored by friendly Arab governments and its European allies, the United States on December 14, 1988, dropped its ban on conducting direct talks with the Palestine Liberation Organization (PLO). This about-face in U.S. diplomacy, taken during the final weeks of the Reagan administration, created both opportunities and problems for President Bush. It opened lines of communication with the Palestinians that presumably would facilitate negotiations. On the other hand, it created potentially unrealistic expectations in the Arab world.

In response to American pressure on Israel to get peace talks moving again after a hiatus of about seven years, Prime Minister Yitzhak Shamir went to Washington April 6, 1989, with a plan to break an impasse resulting from his government's refusal to negotiate with the PLO. He proposed letting Palestinians in Israeli-occupied territories hold elections under Israeli auspices to select representatives to negotiate peace with Israel. Bush promised that the United States would try to enlist Arab support for Shamir's plan—after saying publicly that Israel should end its occupation of the West Bank and Gaza Strip. The

PLO quickly rejected Shamir's plan; Egyptian President Hosni Mubarak, America's closest Arab ally, criticized it but stopped short of rejecting the plan outright.

Reluctant to launch a peace campaign of his own, Bush tried to nudge all sides to the negotiating table. Aside from other, perhaps paramount, reasons for not pushing a Middle East initiative, the president encountered strict limits that Congress had imposed on a president's ability to carry out Middle East policy. Congress had written into law dozens of provisions giving special treatment to Israel and, to a lesser extent, Egypt—in effect, a continuing reward for signing a peace treaty in 1979 at the urging of President Jimmy Carter.

As for the Soviet Union, its pullout from Afghanistan possibly did more than improve Moscow's image in the Middle East. The removal of Soviet forces left a political void in Kabul, the Afghan capital, that might be filled by a regime displeasing to Washington. This would be the situation if the ultimate victor was an Afghan version of the radical fundamentalist regime in Iran. It was also likely that Afghanistan would remain embroiled in years of strife and confusion arising from the inability of any single political or religious group to govern. The weak communist government the Russians left behind was not expected to survive long under sustained attacks by the Mujahedeen rebels, who had been heavily armed by the United States, Iran, and several Arab countries.

The Angola-Namibia accords also left Washington with policy choices. The accords set a timetable for Cuban troop withdrawal from Angola but left unresolved an old conflict between the country's Marxist government and Jonas Savimbi's U.S.-supported insurgents. For the Bush administration, the question would be whether to continue supporting Savimbi if the government did not hold free elections to determine the control of the country or make

some other mutually agreeable arrangement for power sharing.

Central America

Closer to home, Central America remained an object of Washington's concern even if the government spoke "with one voice" on Nicaraguan affairs, as Bush asserted in signing the accord with Congress on contra aid. In El Salvador, the U.S.-backed centrist government was voted out of office March 19, 1989, reducing the prospect of a negotiated settlement with leftist guerrillas and an end to the ten-year-old civil war. And Moscow and Washington had yet to reach a meeting of minds over Nicaragua as they did on Afghanistan and southern Africa. Until a series of cease-fire agreements began in 1988, Soviet-supplied armed forces of Nicaragua's Sandinista government repeatedly clashed with the U.S.-backed guerrillas, the contras, operating from neighboring Honduras. To Reagan, the contras were "freedom fighters." His unabashed enthusiasm for them set him apart from most politicians in Washington. While some conservatives adopted Reagan's rhetoric, most members of Congress never really warmed to the contra cause.

Reagan kept the contra issue alive, forcing more than a dozen major political battles in Congress and leading to the expenditure of more than $250 million in U.S. aid to the contras. But in the face of sustained opposition on Capitol Hill and with his overall influence in Congress lagging, even Reagan ran out of energy. Once the House defeated his 1988 aid request for the contras, he continued to denounce Congress but never again officially asked for more money. Bush never seemed to embrace the contras with the same fervor— although testimony in the trial of Oliver L. North suggested that as vice president he actively participated in undercover efforts to persuade foreign countries to provide

Giving the President a Freer Hand with Foreign Aid

Congress should agree to drop many of its restrictions on the president's use of foreign aid in return for his commitment to work more closely with Capitol Hill, a bipartisan task force of the House Foreign Affairs Committee recommended. In a forty-six-page report released February 1, 1989, the task force severely criticized the current foreign aid program.

The program was so encumbered with restrictions and bureaucratic red tape that it no longer met the goals of protecting U.S. interests and advancing economic development abroad, the report said. The panel recommended scrapping the existing foreign aid law, which was enacted in 1961 and had been amended hundreds of times.

The panel was headed by the second most senior Democratic and Republican members of the committee: Lee H. Hamilton, D-Ind., and Benjamin A. Gilman, R-N.Y. Working behind closed doors for much of 1988, the group held extensive hearings and conducted several staff investigations.

Among the needed changes, the task force said, was a reduction in the conditions and reporting requirements that Congress imposed on the executive branch. The panel noted that current law required the administration to send Congress 288 separate reports on aspects of the foreign aid program.

Congress also had removed much of the administration's flexibility over the amounts of aid to be given specific countries. In fiscal 1989, Congress earmarked 92 percent of all military aid, 98 percent of all economic aid, and 49 percent of all development aid.

"What all this means is that accountability of U.S. foreign assistance is extensive but ineffective," the task force said. The panel noted that, because of congressional restrictions and bureaucratic requirements, "it can take two and a half years to plan and approve a project, by which time conditions have changed and plans need to be revised." The panel said that Congress and the administration should work together to reduce restrictions on the foreign aid program.

Hamilton said he envisioned the two branches striking a deal: "that the executive branch will pay attention to the initiatives of the Congress and not ignore them, and the Congress will not try to micromanage" the foreign aid program. "It's a two-way street."

military aid to the contras during a time when Congress had banned such aid. North, a Marine Corps officer assigned to the national security staff in the White House, was convicted by a federal court jury May 5, 1989, on three felony counts: obstructing Congress, unlawfully mutilating government documents, and taking an illegal gratuity from one of his confederates. He was acquitted of other charges, including the allegation that he lied to Congress about his involvement in a plan to sell arms to Iran and illegally transfer the proceeds to the contras.

During the fall election campaign, Bush did not take a firm stand on restoring U.S. military aid to the contras despite demands by some conservatives that he use it as evidence of Democratic weakness on national security matters. And he portrayed his own role in the Iran-contra affair as inconsequential, saying he was unfamiliar with most of what was occurring. After Bush became president, his secretary of state, Baker, promptly worked out the compromise agreement with both parties in Congress. It was intended to keep the contra force intact in Honduras and put pressure on the Nicaraguan government to hold free elections as they had promised.

Washington and Moscow still remained apart, even as each was expressing peace aims for Central America. Gorbachev, on a visit to Cuba in early April spoke of the need for creating a "zone of peace" in Latin America. The White House said he should put action behind his words and cease arming the Nicaraguan army.

6

The Defense Spending Crunch

A fundamental defense question the Bush administration faced—how big the defense budget would be—at first had a likely answer. Pentagon funding was expected to remain just below the level that President Ronald Reagan requested and Congress approved for fiscal year 1989— about $300 billion, with annual increases sufficient to keep pace with inflation. Bush submitted to Congress comparable spending proposals for fiscal 1990, but the congressional-White House budget accord of April 14, 1989, listed only $305.5 billion in new spending authority for defense during the year—showing an insufficient increase over 1989 to match inflation. What that meant in actual outlays for 1990 was a matter of dispute between Republican and Democratic interpreters.

Congress had refused for several years to consider defense funding except as an element of the overall federal budgetary tangle, which included taxes, deficits, and domestic programs. Since increases in taxes or the budget deficit appeared equally unpopular, a tight lid would remain on domestic programs. With domestic spending essentially frozen, Congress would insist on equivalent treatment for the Pentagon, barring some military threat far more serious than any on the horizon.

Among the first duties of Dick Cheney

upon taking office as secretary of defense on March 17, 1989, was to decide where to cut $6 billion from the defense budget that Bush had ordered. Moreover, Cheney also had to recommend where to lop off some $60 billion from defense spending projected through the mid-1990s. According to defense analysts, this entailed cutting troop levels or weapons procurement, or possibly both. In various public forums, a number of prominent former military and national security officials urged Cheney not to maintain current troop strength at the expense of weapons.

In Reagan's first term, the increased defense funding had concentrated on enhancing what Pentagon officials called the "four pillars" of military strength:

● Force structure: Adding divisions to the Army, carrier task forces to the Navy, and fighter wings to the Air Force.

● Readiness: Training, maintenance, and spare parts.

● Sustainability: Stockpiling ammunition, weapons, equipment for wartime use.

● Modernization: Stepping up production of new ships, planes, tanks, and other essential equipment, and accelerating the effort to develop newer weapons.

The brunt of the post-1985 cutback in defense spending had fallen on procurement, and thus had slowed the pace of modernization. However, the allocations for research and development—the seedbed of future modernization—continued to grow. In 1988 Defense Secretary Frank C. Carlucci submitted the first Reagan defense request that treated tight limits on defense budget growth as a fact of life rather than a passing nuisance. He ordered the armed services to cancel weapons programs and pare back force structure if necessary to avoid cutting back on readiness or sustainability. Most of the weapon cancellations were minor ones. Force-structure cuts were more substantial. But even here, the Navy avoided giving up any major element of its expansion.

Much deeper cuts in planned expenditures would be needed for the Pentagon to squeeze its program into future budgets. Readiness and sustainability had become politically untouchable totems to the most prominent defense specialists of both parties. So as a practical matter the political debate over where to cut was over how much should come out of planned modernization and how much out of force structure.

Strategic Force Issues

There was no indication that Bush disagreed with the rationale underlying Reagan's far-reaching modernization of the nuclear force: the belief that Soviet adventurism was best deterred by a diversified U.S. arsenal that could threaten nuclear attacks of varying degrees of intensity against different kinds of targets. In public discourse, Bush had argued that Reagan's nuclear buildup drove the Russians to the negotiating table. In practical terms, debate over strategic arms funding had focused on two issues:

● Did the United States need a fleet of mobile intercontinental ballistic missiles (ICBMs)? Bush had called for deploying additional ten-warhead MX missiles on rail-road cars. But regardless of the basing method, procurement of any additional MXs would face adamant opposition from liberal arms control activists. For these critics, among them House members such as Thomas J. Downey, D-N.Y., and lobby groups such as Common Cause, the curtailment in 1985 of MX deployments in existing missile silos had been the most tangible victory in seven years of legislative warfare against Reagan's nuclear-arms policies.

● What kind of research on anti-missile defenses should be conducted, and at what cost? Candidate Bush had pledged his support for Reagan's SDI program to develop a nationwide anti-missile defense. Commitment to it had become the touchstone of conservative defense policy. As president, Bush favored a plan outlined in his defense budget that would refocus SDI in a technically and politically risky direction. The budget his defense secretary took to Congress April 25, 1989, revealed that SDI's $4.9 billion fiscal 1990 program was cut down $991 million from Reagan's request. According to Cheney, the Bush team would highlight a relatively new approach to anti-missile defenses called "Brilliant Pebbles." This SDI plan relies on tens of thousands of relatively small interceptor missiles orbiting the Earth, each controlled by a supercomputer the size of a cigarette pack, and each able to destroy a Soviet ICBM in the first few minutes after its launch.

Updating Conventional Forces

The Reagan team justified an across-the-board modernization of conventional forces on two grounds. First, it was making up for modernization that had been deferred because of the cost of fighting the Vietnam War and because of stingy defense budgets resulting from the anti-Pentagon sentiment of the early 1970s. Second, modernization was needed to preserve a technical edge over the more numerous forces of the Soviet Union.

For more than a decade, Pentagon planners had touted a network of airborne detectors and long-range missiles designed to reach miles behind Soviet lines. The network arguably furthered deterrence by threatening to disrupt massed reinforcements that the Soviets might use to roll over Western European defenses worn down by an initial assault. Bush faced a decision on whether to put the costly programs into production.

As for responding to attack, the United States and its NATO allies had gambled that they could blunt a massive Soviet tank assault with guided missiles. The missiles could blast through armor plate with carefully shaped explosive warheads. Such missiles could be launched from simple tripods or jeeps, and thus eliminate the need for huge and costly tanks to challenge the Soviet armor.

However, since 1987 the Soviets had begun rapidly equipping their front-line tanks with a new kind of armor designed to fend off NATO's "shaped-charge" missiles. The Pentagon was exploring new kinds of missiles, and the defense-funding committees in Congress had demanded an accelerated search for answers to the Soviet tank threat.

At sea, the U.S. strategy for dealing with Moscow's huge submarine fleet rested on another technical assumption that had become questionable. The assumption had been that Soviet subs would remain noisy enough to be detected by so-called "passive" sonar—sensitive microphones that would detect subs as far as hundreds of miles away. But newer Soviet subs, which were being built nearly three times as fast as the newest U.S. subs, were proving much quieter than American planners had assumed—partly because of sophisticated manufacturing equipment illegally sold to the Russians by firms in Norway and Japan.

Given the technological challenges and budgetary constraints, congressional critics began focusing on the NATO alliance. Bush faced resentment on Capitol Hill over the substantially smaller defense budgets of America's allies whose security rested in part on the far greater defense effort of the United States. Bush himself called for greater "burden-sharing" by Western Europe and Japan. However, he resisted drastic unilateral steps to achieve this goal, such as significantly reducing the number of U.S. forces overseas.

7

Bush's Unfunded Social Agenda

By promising several new social programs and added funding for others, presidential candidate George Bush put himself in direct conflict with the primary economic objective of President George Bush—that of reducing the federal budget deficit. He asked voters to read his lips when he vowed "no new taxes," but he did not explain what programs he would cut to pay for his campaign promises. In the budget proposals that he sent Congress for fiscal 1990, instead of specifying major domestic cuts he suggested the White House and legislative branch negotiate over what would have to be pared or eliminated.

How to reconcile the conflicting imperatives of increased social spending and deficit reduction, as required by the Gramm-Rudman law, had created a quandary for congressional Democrats throughout Reagan's presidency. Bush faced the same dilemma, because much of his social agenda conformed to the Democrats' agenda. Bush's issues, ranging from health care to child care to help for the homeless, were largely those that first found prominence in Democratic-led Congresses. Indeed, many of the ideas he endorsed on the campaign trail were subsequently enacted into law or moved closer to becoming law.

By advocating increased spending for education, child care, and health services,

candidate Bush moved to close both the "compassion gap" and the "gender gap" with a single stroke. Early on, he sought to distance himself from the Reagan dogma that most social programs should be turned back to the states. Indeed, throughout the fall campaign, Bush had called for immediate infusions of cash for many of the same programs that Reagan tried to cut, including federal grants to college students, child-nutrition and immunization, and Medicaid coverage for poor pregnant women and children.

'How Much Will This Cost?'

"The first thought today in Congress is, 'How much will this cost?'" said House majority leader Thomas S. Foley, D-Wash. "The deficit is an excuse to do nothing on a whole lot of issues." Cost concerns not only dominated debate over social programs, they often dictated policy choices.

However, fiscal constraints did not prove to be an insurmountable obstacle to social initiatives from Congress during the later years of the Reagan administration. Those constraints did not prevent the enactment of a $3.34 billion overhaul of the welfare system in 1988. Democrats also found a way around the deficit to protect Medicare beneficiaries against extremely costly— "catastrophic" —illnesses. They simply put the burden on the beneficiaries, through higher premiums. Other Democratic proposals that were certain to resurface in the 101st Congress would force business to provide health insurance to all workers and require employers to grant workers job-protected leaves-of-absence to care for sick, newborn, or newly adopted children.

Bush, however, opposed efforts to force the business community to pick up the costs for social-policy objectives that the federal government could no longer afford. A health-care position paper issued by the Bush campaign stated that "mandated benefits make low-wage workers proportionately more expensive than other employees. Mandated benefits increase the start-up costs for new businesses—the source of most new job creation—and lessen the flexibility of employers and employees to establish a compensation package that best meets the needs of workers."

If Democrats favored the mandated-benefits approach, Bush seemed to prefer new federal income-tax credits and incentives. He has proposed a tax-credit approach to problems ranging from child care to college savings on the theory that it would give taxpayers the freedom to choose how they wanted to spend their money. But every new tax credit also would drain dollars from the Treasury, worsening the deficit. Republicans and Democrats alike were wary about making major new tax-code changes so soon after the 1986 overhaul of the federal tax system. "It would be nice if we could leave the income-tax system alone for the next four years," said Rep. Bill Gradison, R-Ohio, a member of the House Ways and Means Committee.

In a sense, congressional Democrats had already won the first round in the battle of the social agenda just by getting Bush onto their playing field. The question was no longer whether parents needed time off

from work to spend with their newborn or seriously ill children, but how that goal was to be achieved. No serious debate took place over whether the federal government should aid those without health insurance; the discussion centered on what action the government should take.

Where Reagan often made no proposals on key social-policy issues, entering the fray only in response to Democratic initiatives, Bush would be forced to deal. His only other option would be to publicly disavow his campaign promises. Orrin G. Hatch of Utah, ranking Republican on the Senate Labor and Human Resources Committee, said that if the Democrats' social agenda was fairly moderate, Bush was "going to get along well" with Congress, but he would not "be pushed around by left-wing ideologues" with "radical" social ideas.

Bush "at least acknowledges that there are problems," said Robert Fersh, executive director of the Food Research and Action Center. Bush and Congress might "disagree on how to solve them, but compared with an administration that denied there even was a hunger problem, it's refreshing."

Child Care

The centerpiece of the Bush human-services agenda was a four-part, $2.2 billion child-care plan, unveiled in July 1988 in response to congressional action on a similar proposal. The Bush plan would:

● Create a "children's tax credit" for low-income working families. The refundable credit (which meant that even if the family owed no tax, they still got a "refund") would give low-income families a tax credit of up to $1,000 per child under age four. The credit would be phased in over four years: families with annual incomes below $13,000 would be eligible the first year. Eligibility thresholds would then be phased upward gradually, to between $15,000 and $20,000 annual income by

1994. Bush aides estimated the cost at $1.5 billion the first year, rising to $2.5 billion in fiscal 1993.

● Make the existing dependent-care tax credit refundable. Families could take the larger of the dependent-care tax credit or the new children's credit. Bush aides estimated the cost at $400 million for the first year.

● Require "that every federal agency provide [day-care] assistance to government employees" and establish a federal revolving fund to help private employers who wish to provide day care obtain liability insurance. "Bush does not support using taxpayer dollars to get business to recognize what it already knows: that it must provide assistance for more and better child care," the proposal stated. The estimated cost was $50 million.

● Expand Head Start, the successful preschool education, health, and nutrition program for disadvantaged children aged 3-5. In 1989 about 16 percent of the potentially eligible children were enrolled in Head Start programs. New funding would be phased in gradually, with the aim of ultimately enrolling all eligible four-year-olds. Bush aides estimated the first-year cost at $240 million. Full funding for four-year-olds would cost $2 billion annually, according to an Urban Institute estimate. Appropriations for the whole program in fiscal year 1989 totaled $1.2 billion.

● Provide $10 million in "seed money" for innovative programs for sick-child care, before- and after-school care, and "using educational facilities in innovative and productive ways."

The proposal met with a fairly warm reception from advocates of a nationwide child-care policy. Although skeptical that Bush's proposal was adequate, they welcomed his entry into the debate and said his interest improved their chances of enacting a program.

Upon becoming president, Bush sought

to phase in the child-care package in the fiscal 1990 budget. He requested a $200 million increase over inflation for Head Start. As expected, he proposed to rescind a Reagan budget request to cut $900 million from child nutrition programs, and he promised "full funding" for entitlement programs to assist low-income people.

But the Bush assessment of full funding did not necessarily agree with the Reagan administration's view. For example, Reagan had sought $12.1 billion for the Supplemental Security Income, a Social Security program that provides payments to aged, blind, and disabled individuals with low incomes. Without explanation, the Bush budget sought $11 billion. "There are lots of places where they manipulated the numbers and the effect is to camouflage cuts," said Ellen Nissenbaum of the Center on Budget and Policy Priorities, a Washington-based research group that analyzes funding proposals for the poor.

Most other entitlement programs apparently would be frozen at their 1989 level without allowing for inflation. As in past years, if something was added to one domestic program, then almost always something would be cut from another. But those trade-offs were not spelled out in Bush's initial budget revisions.

Parental Leave

During the presidential campaign, Bush told a group of Republican women in Illinois that giving parents a chance to spend time with their newborn children was important. "We need to assure that women don't have to worry about getting their jobs back after having a child or caring for a child during a serious illness. This is what I mean when I talk about a gentler nation," he said.

The candidate never specified how women would gain such assurance, and he generally opposed mandated benefits.

Nonetheless, Bush's vague commitments spurred congressional Democrats to attempt to pass both minimum-wage and parental-leave legislation in the waning days of the 100th Congress. When their efforts failed, after prolonged Republican-led filibusters in the Senate, the Democrats vowed to put both issues back on the agenda in 1989.

Minimum Wage

If Bush had a labor agenda, it was to counter the same bills—such as a minimum-wage increase and mandated parental-leave policy—that congressional Democrats sought to pass in 1988. But unlike Reagan, who generally refused to negotiate with Congress over those issues, Bush came up with alternatives to the Democrats' plans.

On the campaign trail, in September 1988, Bush had indicated that he would support a slight increase in the minimum wage, then $3.35 an hour. But he never said how big that increase should be. On March 3, 1989, his new labor secretary, Elizabeth H. Dole, unveiled an administration proposal to increase the minimum wage to $4.25 over a three-year period. It would be coupled with a lower training wage for newly hired workers; employers would not have to pay them more than $3.35 an hour during their first six months on the job.

"Legislation outside of these parameters would call for a veto," Dole warned at a hearing before the Senate Labor and Human Resources Committee. The warning challenged Edward M. Kennedy, D-Mass., the committee's chairman, who had introduced legislation to raise the wage to $4.65 an hour, without a training-wage proposal. Rep. Augustus F. Hawkins, D-Calif., Kennedy's counterpart in the House, called the administration's plan "absolutely absurd."

By mid-April both the House and Senate had passed similar bills to phase in a $3.55-an-hour minimum wage by October 1, 1991, and set a subminimum wage floor at 15 percent less. Though passed by sizable majorities in both chambers, neither bill received the two-thirds vote that would be required to override a Bush veto.

Housing the Homeless

In his fiscal 1990 budget revisions, Bush sought to keep a campaign promise to "fully fund" the Stewart B. McKinney Homeless Assistance Act, a 1987 law named for a Connecticut representative who died of AIDS complications. Bush proposed to add $336 million to the amount Reagan had requested, thus bringing discretionary spending under the emergency-aid act to the $676 million-level that Congress had authorized. Bush's budget requests for all forms of homeless assistance came to just more than $1 billion, some $407 million more than Reagan requested.

Democrats and some urban Republicans in Congress said they welcomed Bush's intention to spend more for the homeless, but they also wanted to see a reversal of the Reagan-era trend that siphoned money away from low-income housing construction. "It's better than nothing, better than Ronald Reagan, no doubt about it, but not nearly good enough," said Rep. Barney Frank, D-Mass., an outspoken liberal. "He's going to do a lot for the homeless, but he's not going to see that they get any homes."

The key to housing the nation better, Bush said repeatedly during the campaign, was "a strong economy" that would permit low mortgage rates and a healthy home-building industry. Reagan had used the same argument to curtail government spending on housing. To increase the supply of low-rent housing for the very poorest, Bush favored short-term rent subsidies over construction grants and tax breaks. These so-called rent "vouchers," a major tenet of Reagan's policies, were rooted in a basic conservative belief—that the country's housing problem was mostly one of affordability, not availability.

However, a campaign paper dated September 22, 1988, implied that Bush would not be so adverse to construction subsidies as Reagan had been. "George Bush's housing policy," the paper stated, "is flexible enough to address local areas where housing availability is a real problem. Under George Bush, the federal government will support local initiatives to build more housing." In addition to supporting emergency-aid programs in the McKinney Act, Bush called for increasing the limits on federally insured mortgages and lowering the down payments required of borrowers.

For him, the trick would be relieving low-income housing shortages with a lean housing budget. Housing experts predicted that shortages of low-rent housing units, which already had occurred in many urban areas, would spread even further. Their predictions were based on the expectation that many owners of projects built with government aid during the past two decades would be able to convert their property to more profitable uses as subsidies and restrictions expired.

Estimates differed widely over how many of the two million privately owned, government-subsidized units were really at risk. The National Low Income Housing Preservation Commission concluded from a 1988 analysis that as many as one million units could be lost within the next fifteen years. "By 2003, the gap between the total low-rent housing supply and households needing such housing is projected to grow to 7.8 million units," according to a study by Phillip L. Clay of the Massachusetts Institute of Technology. HUD responded that Clay "vastly overstates the nature of the problem," but it added, "Obviously, there is much still to be done."

Attempts to spend money to build new housing or extend expiring subsidies would have to be balanced with the dire needs of the government's biggest shelter investment—1.4 million units of existing public housing. Some cost estimates for needed repairs to those units went up to $20 billion, though the government figure was much smaller. One potential source of money was available to pay for such housing programs. Some members of Congress looked to removing or limiting the mortgage-interest deduction for homeowners in the tax code for increased revenue. Homeowners get various tax breaks—estimated to be worth more than $50 billion in fiscal 1989 alone, compared with the less than $30 billion the government would spend on various low-income housing programs.

But it was extremely unlikely that Congress would scale back home-ownership tax breaks, especially with pressure mounting to help first-time home buyers. Any attempt to do so would draw heated objections from the nation's most influential housing interest groups—the realtors, the home builders, and the mortgage bankers—not to mention the country's most powerful political force, the middle class.

8

Financing Ever-Costlier Health Care

Death and taxes might be inevitable, but a dearth of both was fueling a health-care crisis that experts predicted the Bush administration would be forced to address. The federal government has an enormous stake in the cost of health care. In fiscal 1987 Medicare and Medicaid, the two big health-insurance programs for the elderly and the poor, respectively, accounted for $117 billion—11.6 percent of all federal outlays. Only Social Security and defense cost more. And costs for Medicare and Medicaid were rising far more rapidly than for other major programs. Between 1989 and 1990, for example, costs for Medicare and Medicaid were expected to jump by 13 percent, from $131 billion to $148 billion.

Facing a huge and intractable budget deficit, President Bush had to tackle the problem of ever-rising health-care costs if he was to make even modest headway in stemming the tide of red ink. And he had to do so at a time when Americans were demanding more—not less—federal help with health costs, especially for the elderly and chronically ill.

The expanding costs resulted, in part, because people were not dying as soon as they used to. In 1940, only 7.4 percent of those who reached age sixty-five could be expected to live to age ninety. By 1980, 24.5 percent could. Even if no further progress

was made toward extending old age, the 85-and-older group would make up nearly one-fourth of the elderly population by the year 2050; they accounted for only 10 percent in 1987. Older people need more health care than others. Senior citizens were only 12 percent of the population in 1987, but they accounted for more than a third of the nation's annual bill for personal health care.

Many of the same technological breakthroughs that were helping people live longer were also helping to drive up health-care costs faster than those of any other sector of the economy. In 1986, the cost of medical care rose by 7.5 percent, compared with a 1.9 percent increase in the overall Consumer Price Index. Since 1979, health costs had increased faster than overall price increases, and since 1982, faster than housing, energy, and other segments of the economy.

Even more ominous to many analysts was the growing percentage of the nation's gross national product that was consumed by health care: 10.9 percent in 1986, up from 8.5 percent in 1976 and 6 percent in 1966. "Americans spent almost $1,800 a person on health care in 1985—far more than Canadians, who ranked second ($1,300), more than twice the Japanese ($800), and triple the British ($600)," Joseph A. Califano, Jr., secretary of health, education, and welfare under President Jimmy Carter, told the congressional Joint Economic Committee in May 1988. "Yet health care in Canada, Japan, and Britain is sophisticated and modern, life expectancy is at least as high as in the United States, and infant mortality is lower."

Daniel R. Waldo of the Health Care Financing Administration (HCFA) testified before the same committee: "[A]s we continue to reduce the rate of 'low cost' sudden deaths—from cardiovascular disease and so on—it means that more people will be dying from the expensive diseases such as cancer. In addition, a fair amount of medical care is spent not in prolonging life but in prolonging death."

America's litigious nature was another factor contributing to rising prices, analysts said. Not only did the cost of medical care reflect the increased price of professional liability insurance, but more health professionals were practicing "defensive medicine" —ordering tests or doing procedures not considered absolutely necessary—lest they be held responsible later in court for what is euphemistically referred to in the medical community as "a bad outcome."

It is difficult for patients to know what is necessary and what is not in health care. "Health care is one of those strange markets in which consumers must rely heavily upon suppliers to determine the extent of demand," Waldo said. Yet another factor, suggested some, was the fault of patients themselves. "Patients have come to judge physicians by how much doctors do to them—how spectacular their diagnostic and treatment procedures are, how high-tech their offices and hospitals are," said Califano. "We must re-educate patients, promoting a cultural shift in patient attitudes."

Web of Connections

Health-care costs were so interrelated that dropping a stone in one portion of the vast pool caused ripples in other portions. For example, when the federal Medicare program imposed new rules in 1983 aimed at curbing hospital costs, bills for outpatient services began to escalate rapidly. Pressing down on one side of a balloon only seemed to make another side bulge.

In 1989 pressure was mounting on Capitol Hill and in the executive branch for curbs, direct or indirect, on physicians' fees. But proposals to rein in the number of federal dollars that wind up in the pockets of doctors raised as many problems as they sought to solve. Two truisms need to be considered when attempting to address cost issues, Califano said: "[W]hen we tinker with any part of this supplier-controlled behemoth, we affect all parts of it; and medical services follow reimbursement dollars the way an alley cat follows the scent of fish in the garbage."

Another difficulty inherent in the cost issue involved determining exactly what constituted appropriate or "quality" medical care. "It has become clear that we cannot contain costs intelligently unless we know what it is we get for our money," said Arnold S. Relman, editor in chief of the *New England Journal of Medicine* and a noted health policy authority. "We need to understand what the outcomes are of what we do. New technology is being introduced more rapidly than we have time to evaluate it."

According to Relman, the nation was about to embark on the third health-care revolution since World War II. The first, he said, began in the late 1940s, when employer-provided health insurance became the norm, and continued through the mid-1960s, when the federal government extended basic coverage to the elderly and poor with Medicare and Medicaid. That vastly expanded stream of funding helped drive the inflationary spiral higher and spawned the cost-containment era of the late 1970s and early 1980s. Relman described this time as "the revolt of the payers" —employers, insurance companies and the government—who "suddenly woke up to the fact that they were going to go broke if they simply continued to pay the bills."

That revolt gave rise, in turn, to such now-commonplace requirements as getting a second opinion before surgery and to the proliferation of fixed-price health-maintenance organizations and preferred-provider plans. Relman believed a third stage was at hand. "It's beginning to dawn on payers that we need to establish some system of assessment." Continued inflation, he said, was part of "the price we pay for a lack of hard, systematic evidence of the effectiveness of new technology and new drugs."

Cutting back, though, forced policy makers to face the political taboo: saying "no" to certain forms of health care. For instance, when the Oregon Legislature in 1987 halted Medicaid coverage of organ transplants in order to fund basic health care for more low-income pregnant women and infants, public anguish at the plight of families suddenly denied transplants for dying children ultimately forced a partial retreat. The key question was, Relman continued, "How are we going to contain costs without applying Draconian measures that will result in rationing or arbitrary denial of services?"

New Demands Looming

The basic structure of the U.S. healthcare system had remained virtually intact since 1965, when Medicare and Medicaid were created. But even as the system staggered under the costs of existing demand, new pressures were building. The Bush administration would have to deal with one or more of the following:

• Upwards of thirty-seven million Americans had no health insurance, yet some two-thirds of them worked full-time or were dependents of full-time workers. "I don't care what the political bent is, when you have a nation with [that many] uninsured, that has to be an issue," said Jeffrey Merrill, vice president of the Robert Wood Johnson Foundation, one of the pre-eminent funders of health-policy studies. "It's kind of a festering sore," said health analyst Jack Meyer. The problem had been largely ignored in the past, because hospitals in particular were able to pass on the costs of free charity care to other patients and their insurance companies. But as the federal government and private insurance companies tried to ratchet down their costs, hospitals were running out of ways to pass on unreimbursed costs. And patient "dumping," the practice of turning away uninsured patients, had reached such proportions Congress had sought to forbid it by law.

• Relman described long-term care as "a crying issue that must be dealt with. We do not have an adequate care system for the chronically ill and debilitated. The only federal support is Medicaid, and to be eligible for Medicaid, you have to be a pauper and your spouse does, too. It is not a viable arrangement."

Congressional debate over the Medicare "catastrophic" coverage bill (PL 100-360) in 1988 helped inform millions of the nation's elderly that Medicare did not cover long-term care expenses, and that they (and their families) were at very real financial risk should they need to enter a nursing home.

"Politically there's more people pushing for it," said Karen Davis of the Johns Hopkins University School of Public Health. "The issue has certainly come to the forefront." At the same time, the costs of long-term care were astronomical. The House in 1988 shied away from a proposal to pay for home-based care for the chronically ill—at an estimated cost of at least $28 billion over four years. To cover nursing-home care, which most viewed as a greater need, would be even more expensive.

● While most of the policy debate over AIDS (acquired immune deficiency syndrome) had centered on issues of testing and research, the lingering question was how the bill would be paid. A study by the Department of Health and Human Services (HHS) in 1988 predicted that the treatment bill for those suffering from AIDS could top $4.5 billion in 1991 alone.

Many AIDS patients found themselves without jobs or the health insurance coverage they used to take for granted, yet few could afford treatment costs for the fatal disease, a tab that averages some $57,000 per person.

Bush's Approach

Underlying Bush's approach to health policy, according to Deborah Steelman, his principal social-policy adviser in the presidential election campaign, was a single overriding question: "Why are we spending 11 percent of our gross national product on health, and what are we getting for it?" What we were not getting was universal access to health care.

Health-policy experts and lawmakers alike had grown increasingly concerned about the plight of an estimated 37 million Americans who lack any type of health-insurance coverage.

Democratic presidential nominee Michael S. Dukakis hammered on the issue, calling for nationwide expansion of a new Massachusetts law requiring most employers to provide their workers with health insurance. Congress was already moving in that direction. The Senate Labor and Human Resources Committee in February 1988 approved a bill similar to the Dukakis plan, and Chairman Edward M. Kennedy, D-Mass., chief sponsor of the measure, intended to press it again in 1989. That

approach, however, was anathema to most of the business community and to Bush, who firmly opposed mandated benefits.

Bush preferred a plan, originated by Sen. John H. Chafee, R-R.I., to allow the low-income uninsured to "buy into" Medicaid, the joint state-federal health program for the very poor, but Bush campaign aides released few details about how such a plan would work. Bush criticized the Dukakis plan for not addressing the needs of the unemployed uninsured. But a study by the nonpartisan Employee Benefit Research Institute (EBRI) concluded that the Bush proposal could be as expensive as the Dukakis plan and would serve fewer people. Under the Dukakis plan, costs would be borne by businesses; under the Bush proposal, most of the cost would fall on the federal and state governments.

The two approaches for dealing with the problem were not mutually exclusive. In fact, the American Public Welfare Association (APWA) recommended a policy encompassing elements of both. "While researchers, analysts and lawmakers have proposed either a broadened Medicaid program or mandated employer coverage, APWA believes that the only way to equitably address the problems of those lacking health insurance is to implement both proposals," said an APWA report. Acknowledging that such changes would be costly, the report said, "It is important to keep in mind, however, that this nation is already incurring far greater social and economic costs through continued inaction."

Bush also wanted to encourage small businesses to offer insurance to their employees. "Helping small employers gain information about their health-insurance options and facilitating their grouping together to purchase insurance at lower prices are strategies that should be explored before turning to an anti-competitive measure like mandated benefits," said a Bush position paper. But Steelman said that giving unincorporated businesses the same tax advantages for providing insurance that corporations enjoy "is simply too expensive." She cautioned that medical coverage for the uninsured was "a long-term goal," indicating that ten years would not be unrealistic.

In his budget proposals, Bush sought to restore all but $352 million of the $1.7 billion that Reagan wanted to cut from Medicaid funds in fiscal 1990 and at the same time asked Congress to reduce Medicare costs by $5 billion. Most of the Medicare savings Bush envisioned would result from going along with three Reagan budget proposals: decrease reimbursements for hospital capital spending, lower Medicare's special contribution to teaching hospitals, and continue a "temporary" rule imposed in 1982 (and extended each year since) requiring that beneficiary premiums pay at least 25 percent of the cost of the program's optional Part B, which covers doctor bills. Many members of Congress were skeptical that such savings could be achieved. "There's no way that we could take $5 billion out of Medicare," said Rep. Dan Rostenkowski, D-Ill., chairman of the House Ways and Means Committee.

Child Health

In asking Congress to restore most of the Medicaid cuts that Reagan wanted, Bush was moving forward on a campaign pledge to improve the health of the nation's children. The restored Medicaid funds would provide services to pregnant women and to infants up to one year old in families with income below 130 percent of the federally defined poverty threshold—widening the federal law that cuts off at 100 percent but falling short of the 185 percent figure that Bush had mentioned on the campaign trail. Moreover, his plan would extend Medicaid coverage for immunizations against childhood diseases for all children up to age five who were eligible for food stamps.

In line with proposals by the business-led Committee for Economic Development (CED) and the Democratic-controlled Congress, candidate Bush called for increased Medicaid coverage for poor pregnant women and young children. He then had urged mandatory Medicaid coverage for all children in families with incomes at or below the poverty level, as well as coverage for unspecified numbers of children in families with incomes up to 185 percent of the poverty level. He had vowed to spend up to $400 million in fiscal 1990 to begin his phase-in.

EBRI had estimated that to extend Medicaid to the 4.6 million older children in those same families who remained uninsured would cost some $2.3 billion. Still, advocates for children's health programs were upbeat. "The Bush proposal is certainly a step in the right direction, certainly part of a solution," said Sara Rosenbaum, director of health programs for the Children's Defense Fund (CDF). Nor did advocates disagree with Bush advisers who said that programs such as Medicaid and the Women, Infants, and Children (WIC) nutrition program need to be expanded gradually. Because of the potential for overloading the system, WIC advocates such as the Food Research and Action Center (FRAC) wanted to increase funding by some $250 million a year for four years to reach the additional $1 billion needed to serve all those potentially eligible for the program. In 1989, the program was funded at $1.9 billion and served an estimated 3.7 million individuals.

AIDS Epidemic

On key issues involved in the government's response to the AIDS epidemic, Bush distanced himself from Reagan. Unlike Reagan, he endorsed federal legislation to protect the carriers of HIV, the virus that causes AIDS, from discrimination. Testing and contact-tracing programs, Bush told reporters on June 28, 1988, "will be ineffective without being coupled with strict confidentiality and anti-discrimination provisions." Asked whether the issue was best left to the states—at the time, the administration's official position—Bush replied, "I think you have a national problem, and therefore I think there is some national, federal responsibility."

Bush's support of broad anti-discrimination legislation put him on a collision course with some congressional conservatives, notably Sen. Jesse Helms, R-N.C., and Rep. William E. Dannemeyer, R-Calif. But it was welcomed by influential Democrats on Capitol Hill. Bush also was likely to be more in tune with Congress than Reagan was over AIDS funding. The thrust of Bush's program to help the poor, Bush aide Richard Porter told a forum on the disadvantaged in October 1988, was "to make government aid more accessible and deliver it better. We want to target assistance and, at the same time, foster economic growth . . . to put more of the poor into the work force."

In his fiscal 1990 budget, Bush proposed $1.6 billion for AIDS research, education, and testing programs. That was $313 million more than Reagan proposed but $300 million less than Otis R. Bowen, Reagan's HHS secretary, said was needed.

Long-Term Care

One very visible health issue on which Bush promised little was long-term health care. Because of its massive price tag, such care was not covered by the 1988 catastrophic-insurance law. In 1987 the Washington-based Villers Foundation offered each major Democratic and Republican presidential candidate an individual forum to discuss the issue with New Hampshire voters. The only candidates who did not accept were Bush and Democrat Gary Hart.

Given the political clout of the elderly, Bush did not ignore the issue altogether, although he described the problem as primarily a "matter of education," suggesting that the elderly should be taught to save for potential long-term care costs. But he had endorsed changing the tax code to provide incentives for those who could afford it to purchase group long-term care insurance. And he had promised to provide "adequate funding" for research into diseases that result in the need for long-term care, including Alzheimer's disease, osteoporosis, and stroke.

Congressional Democrats considered such proposals inadequate to deal with the long-term care problem, but they had been stymied in their attempts to find a solution the government and the elderly could afford. A fairly modest bill introduced in the 100th Congress by Sen. George J. Mitchell, D-Maine, who became the Senate majority leader in the 101st Congress, would cost an estimated $20 billion per year. Most of that amount would come from increased taxes and premiums paid by the elderly. More ambitious plans offered by other legislators carried price tags closer to $50 billion per year.

9

The 'Education President'

While trekking across New Hampshire during January 1988 in quest of the Republican nomination, George Bush came out with one of his campaign's lasting catch phrases. "I want to be the education president," he told a group of students at Manchester High School. It would be no easy task, however, for President Bush to fill in the blanks of the candidate's sweeping promise.

During the campaign, he had proposed full funding for programs such as Head Start for disadvantaged preschool children and Pell Grants for college students. He had called for plans to encourage low- and middle-income families to save money for their children's college and vocational education. To foster competition and quality teaching, he had proposed giving bonuses or other special recognition to the country's best schools and teachers. He had told campaign audiences that a Bush administration would stop the erosion in education funding.

"I can say unequivocally that I will not support any further cuts in total federal funding for education. We can spend more wisely, but we must not spend less," Bush told the New Hampshire students. But he added a cautionary note in a speech to another audience five months later. "When it comes to better schools, almost all of the wisdom and the good answers and the money to pay the bills should come from outside Washington, D.C."

The new president went before Congress on February 9 with a set of sketchy budget proposals estimated to add $441 million to the $21.9 billion in education spending that Reagan had requested. He provided more details at a press conference April 5, and congressional Republicans immediately introduced the package of proposals in legislative form to provide the following in fiscal 1990:

• $250 million to reward "merit schools" for fighting illegal drugs, preventing dropouts, and raising student achievement.

• $100 million for "magnet schools" that seek to attract students by offering special programs.

• $25 million in grants to the states for certifying professionals who had not been trained to teach.

• $25 million to urban schools to fight severe drug problems among their students.

• $7.6 million for teacher excellence awards, worth $5,000 each.

• $5 million for college scholarships to 570 high school seniors showing the most promise in science and math.

• $10 million for endowment grants to historically black colleges.

• $18 million for various education initiatives.

51

Rep. Augustus F. Hawkins, D-Calif., chairman of the House Education and Labor Committee, accused Bush of "attempting to strip programs long supported in Congress to pay for new initiatives of questionable value." Rep. Bill Goodling, R-Pa., the committee's ranking minority member, who had advised Bush during the election campaign, said he shared some of the same concerns.

"We will have to work this into a package that will help us get the revenue we need for these programs and existing programs," Goodling said in an interview.

Bush's Campaign Proposals

As spelled out during the campaign and later, Bush said that successful experiments in Harlem and in the state of Minnesota had persuaded him to "encourage" other states and local communities to set up "open enrollment" programs that allowed parents to choose which public schools their children would attend. Theoretically, if public schools had to compete for students, they would improve the quality of education.

Bush would retarget federal Chapter 1 grants, which were doled out to school districts serving a high proportion of poor students. Bush campaign literature contended that nearly 60 percent of the students who received Chapter 1 aid were not disadvantaged.

As for rewarding schools whose students improved most, the states would determine how to measure academic success. Outstanding schools would be called "National Merit Schools" and those educating many disadvantaged students would get bonuses.

Bush's aides estimated that the program could cost up to $500 million annually if 20 percent of the schools serving poor students—5,000—qualified for the award. His budget proposals included a start on this program.

Bush promised more money for the Fund for Innovation and Reform of Schools and Teaching (FIRST). The fund aimed at fostering experimentation—such as merit pay for teachers and year-round education—at the local level. Congress appropriated $5.9 million for it in fiscal year 1989.

To help families save for college, Bush said on the campaign trail that he would push for legislation enabling persons with incomes up to $80,000 to receive tax-free interest on U.S. savings bonds if the interest was used for tuition. The 100th Congress beat Bush to the draw, approving the savings-bond plan late in 1988.

Bush proposed full funding for Pell Grants to needy college students and government-guaranteed student loans. Ironically, the Reagan administration repeatedly had tried to slash Pell Grant funding and limit eligibility for student loans.

"I want to cut the dropout rate, and make America a more literate nation," Bush said in his 1989 budget speech to Congress *(See* Budget Address to Congress, *in the appendix, p. 111.)* "Because what it really comes down to is this: The longer our graduation lines are today, the shorter our unemployment lines will be tomorrow." At that time, one-fourth of all students were dropping out before high school graduation—with the dropout rate highest among blacks, Hispanics, and Native Americans.

Trends indicated that nearly one-third of all school-age children would be minorities—black, Hispanic, Native American, and Asian—by the year 2000, 42 percent of the children in public schools would be minority, poor, or both, and a majority of those children would be at risk of dropping out of school. Others might graduate but be unable to afford college. Some might not have the skills to hold a job. Already, up to twenty-three million adults lacked basic reading, writing, and math skills, and many businesses had started remedial education classes for their workers.

Future Education Needs

Studies indicated that more than half of the new jobs created after 1989 would require some form of post-secondary education. The future work force would need to know how to use computers, lasers, and other high-technology tools. There would be a shrinking pool of jobs that required little or no skills. "If these kids have no skills, no jobs, what do you think they'll be doing?" asked Bob Hochstein of the Carnegie Foundation for the Advancement of Teaching. "They'll be hitting us over the head. There will be mayhem."

The American Council on Education (ACE), in a forty-nine-page "Memorandum to the 41st President of the United States," advocated the development of business-education partnerships, incentives for families to save money for their children's education, and international exchanges for students and teachers alike. The National School Boards Association, in a pre-election plea to the next president, focused on the plight of elementary and secondary schools. The board recommended upgrading science, math, and technology programs; pro-viding competitive grants for teachers to encourage better instruction of at-risk students; and creating a "second chance" program for high school dropouts.

The Education Testing Service of Princeton, N.J., in one of its periodic assessments of American education, issued a report February 14, 1989, saying that the public schools would have to raise their sights and standards. The study, titled "Crossroads of American Education," concluded that "fundamental changes" would be required in the way schools teach and students learn.

In 1983 Terrel H. Bell, then the secretary of education, warned of a "rising tide of mediocrity that threatens our very future as a nation and a people. . . . We have, in effect, been committing an act of unthinking, unilateral educational disarmament." His report was titled, "A Nation at Risk." His highly critical assessment of the nation's education system stimulated a smattering of school reform at the state and local level. But five years after it was published, another education secretary, William J. Bennett, concluded in another report that "We are still at risk."

10

Environmental Issues: Breaking with Reagan

By 1989 Congress had spent much of the past two decades enacting an ever-tighter group of environmental laws, and the Environmental Protection Agency (EPA) estimated it had more than half a decade's work left to do in carrying out some of these regulations. In addition, EPA was conducting numerous environmental studies that were under similar deadlines.

The studies had been ordered by the Reagan administration, whose approach to environmental problems was to study them. The studies included the effects of pesticides on human health, pesticide contamination of groundwater, trace toxic pollutants in drinking water, and radon and other indoor air pollution. As those studies ended and yielded recommendations, President George Bush would be called on to act.

Moreover, "community right-to-know" provisions of the 1986 "superfund" law, passed to finance the cleanup of toxic-waste sites, gave communities a right to know what dangerous chemicals a nearby industrial plant was using or routinely emitting. These provisions, which became effective late in 1988, were likely to result in a public clamor for more federal enforcement and legislation.

During the presidential campaign,

Bush promised to do more environmental issues such as controlling ocean dumping and acid rain and cleaning up toxic-waste sites. Bush also promised to take the lead in preserving wetlands. He spoke repeatedly of environmental concerns, and in several attacks on Democratic candidate Michael S. Dukakis, Bush called attention to the pollution in Boston harbor.

As president, Bush named a conservationist, William K. Reilly, to administer the EPA. On the other hand, he appointed former Rep. Manuel Lujan, Jr., R-N.M., who as a lawmaker often opposed environmental legislation, to be secretary of the interior. Given his legislative record, some environmentalists expressed concern that he would be the one in charge of national parks and forests and other vast portions of the federal domain. *(See The Cabinet, p. 67).*

One of Reilly's first acts as EPA administrator was cheered by environmentalists. He blocked a regional office's approval of plans for a big dam across the South Platte River in Colorado. Denver officials said the proposed Twin Fork Dam was vital to the metropolitan area's future water needs. It was opposed by environmentalists who argued that water backed up by the dam would destroy a scenic canyon and deprive valuable downstream wetlands of water. Reilly's decision, the *New York Times* said in an editorial page comment, sent a message that "he intends to run his own agency. He takes at face value President Bush's announced concerns for the environment."

Reilly assumed a post that had lost much of its credibility and stature over the past eight years. During the Reagan administration, the EPA's laissez-faire attitude toward environmental law enforcement led to continual clashes between the agency and environmental groups, and often with Congress.

Reilly was president of the Conservation Foundation, a small environmental policy think tank, and of the American affiliate of the World Wildlife Fund, an activist group devoted to saving the natural resources of developing nations. His practice had been to follow a middle course—carefully cultivating the cooperation of business while keeping an ear tuned to environmentalists' voices.

"I have given most of my career to the effort to try to promote consensus between the interests concerned with development and those concerned for the protection of the environment," Reilly said upon being named the agency's director. His interest in consensus-building had occasionally led some environmentalists to question his commitment to using the power of government to clean up the environment. An example was the Conservation Foundation's involvement in an EPA-sponsored study to reevaluate the "superfund" hazardous-waste cleanup law, which Ronald Reagan signed reluctantly in 1986.

Some environmentalists maintained that "superfund" needed tough enforcement, not amending, and that Reilly should not participate in any effort to change the law. However, most environmentalists praised Reilly and dismissed such objections as quibbles about his purity. "He kept his organization in the fold as a bona fide environmental group while maintaining a good relationship with industry," said J. Michael McCloskey, chairman of the Sierra Club.

Reilly pointed out that he was the first EPA administrator to be plucked directly from an environmental group. Some industry representatives privately expressed surprise at the choice. But it did not deter the Senate from approving his appointment by a vote of 100-0 on February 2, 1989.

Reilly said Bush had assured him that he would sit on the Domestic Policy Council, and that "I will be in the cabinet room whenever issues touch on the environment." He noted that he had attended the first meeting of Bush's cabinet.

Acid-Rain Turnabout

In his first address to Congress on February 9, 1989, Bush said: "I will send to you shortly legislation for a new, more effective Clean Air Act. It will include a plan to reduce, by date certain, the emissions which cause acid rain—because the time for study alone has passed, and the time for action is now."

The following day, in his first presidential visit abroad, Bush repeated his acid-rain pledge in Ottawa, Canada, a country that had long clamored for U.S. action on acid rain. For years, Canadian officials had charged that airborne pollutants from American industries were harming the lakes and forests of Canada's eastern provinces. At a press conference in the Canadian capital, Bush said he could not commit himself to a timetable for congressional action on acid rain, but "the prime minister [Brian Mulroney] once again impressed on me the urgency for moving as fast as we can. . . ."

Reagan had sought to deflect concerns over acid rain by saying not enough was known about it to justify a program of mandatory controls that would cost American industry billions of dollars. He staved off demands for immediate controls by launching a national research program at a cost of more than $300 million. The ten-year program was scheduled to report findings in 1990.

The key source of sulfur dioxide, which causes acid rain, was coal-burning electric power plants, especially those in the upper Midwest and Ohio Valley. Acid-rain politics were more regional than partisan. States such as West Virginia that mine high-sulfur coal opposed acid-rain controls, fearing loss of business. States downwind of the smokestacks—principally those in the Northeast—blamed the acid rain for killing fish and forests and demanded existing controls on sulfur dioxide be tightened.

American coal-fired power plants emitted a small but significant portion, about 7 percent, of all man-made carbon dioxide worldwide. The growing concern over global warming could change the regional politics of acid rain, because a cure for the one was tied to the other—raising pressure to burn less coal, burn it more efficiently, and turn to cleaner-burning fuels such as natural gas. Hundreds of millions of dollars were already appropriated to finance the commercialization of Clean Coal Technology, as it is called. Coal-producing states would ask for more federal funds. Many of those technologies would also help with carbon dioxide emissions.

Clean-Air Struggle

Despite the expressions of public support for cleaner air, Congress had been divided, unsure whether the people were willing to accept, or could afford, the economic consequences of air-quality standards that were stringent enough to protect their health and environment. Big cities continued to miss deadlines set by the law for meeting federal standards on carbon monoxide and ozone. The heart of the Clean Air Act enacted in 1970 had been the attempt to control urban smog. That law required automobile manufacturers to install catalytic converters to curb tailpipe emissions.

Although auto industry spokesmen said the control devices had eliminated 96 percent of the carbon monoxide emissions, some forty million Americans still lived in cities and suburbs that exceeded federal air-quality standards for carbon monoxide; seventy-five million lived in areas that violated the standard for ozone, another component of smog. Ozone forms a protective layer in the upper atmosphere, shielding life on Earth from harmful solar rays. But close to the ground, ozone is a pervasive air contaminant. It forms when nitrogen oxides and volatile organic compounds react chemically in the presence of oxygen and sunlight.

Unusual heat in the summer of 1988—the year's overall temperatures were the highest ever recorded worldwide—made the smog worse than previously recorded in several American cities. That heat, many scientists suspected, was a symptom of the "greenhouse effect" or the global warming of the atmosphere. Man-made gases were starting to act like glass in a greenhouse, trapping solar heat and raising the Earth's temperature. These gases were carbon dioxide that resulted from deforestation and the industrial burning of fossil fuels, especially coal. Moreover, chlorofluorocarbons (CFCs), chemicals produced in the manufacture of foamed plastics and air-conditioning systems, were implicated in the destruction of the protective layer of ozone in the stratosphere.

The control of air pollutants in and above the Earth would require measures far more stringent than merely putting anti-pollution devices on tailpipes and smokestacks. It might mean switching fuels, burning them more efficiently, and eventually eliminating fossil fuels such as coal and petroleum. It might mean serious consideration of global population planning. And it might signal the beginning of a new era of environmental problems that required global rather than national solutions.

More than thirty countries, including the United States, had ratified a 1987 agreement to halve their production of CFCs by the end of the century. In an effort to end their manufacture entirely, Britain's Prime Minister Margaret Thatcher convened a conference of 123 countries in London in March 1989. Twenty additional countries said they would abide by the reduction agreement, but Thatcher was unable to get the conference participants to agree to a timetable for a worldwide ban on CFC production.

Oil-Spill Politics

Bush, a former Texas oilman, sided with the oil industry in its fight with conservationists for permission to drill for oil on the Arctic National Wildlife Refuge in Alaska. In his February 9 speech to Congress, the president said drilling could be conducted there without endangering wildlife or damaging the region's fragile ecology. But the oil industry's efforts to win congressional approval for that drilling suffered a severe setback on March 24. On that day the oil tanker *Exxon Valdez* ran aground off the Alaskan coast and spilled ten million gallons of crude oil into Prince William Sound, creating the worst disaster of its kind ever to occur in American waters. Under the Alaska National Interest Lands Act, the refuge on Alaska's north slope has wilderness status unless Congress permits development. Legislation to permit drilling was shelved in the oil spill's aftermath.

As with past environmental disasters, the *Valdez* spill was seen by some as a tragic aberration that should not alter fundamental energy policy, and by others as the inevitable consequence of an energy policy that desperately needed reform. Expressing the first view, Bush said at a press conference April 7 that he had not changed his mind about the the need for drilling on the Alaskan wildlife refuge. "I don't think you can predicate a sound national energy policy on an aberration that seemed to have taken place in Prince William Sound.... I am not going to suggest, because of this, we should rethink a policy of trying to get this country less dependent on foreign oil ...." Voicing another view, Rep. Mel Levine, D-Calif., called on the Bush administration to cancel all pending oil-lease sales off the coast of California. A 1969 oil spill in Santa Barbara harbor had been the nation's worst until the Alaskan accident occurred.

In the February 9 address to Congress, Bush balanced his support for Alaskan drilling by saying he would postpone the government's sale of oil and gas leases for drilling off the California coast and in the vicinity of the Florida Everglades. His decision on whether to move ahead with leasing the sites would await the conclusions of a special task force set up to measure the potential for environmental damage.

Environmental matters often become entwined in energy-policy and national-security questions. After the Arab oil embargo of 1973-74, President Jimmy Carter set out on a quest for "energy independence" —seeking to eliminate this nation's dependence on foreign energy supplies, especially on imported oil. This goal, though never formally renounced, was effectively discarded by official policy in the 1980s. Oil imports again flowed unimpeded to American shores. Energy conservation and alternative energy sources such as water, wind, and sun—all promoted by Carter—found no favor with President Reagan. Subsidies for their development fell victim to severe budget reductions and Reagan's emphasis on oil, coal, and nuclear energy. All three energy sources received billions of dollars in tax benefits or other subsidies.

Nevertheless, conservation measures that had been instilled in or imposed on Americans did hold down the nation's total energy use for more than a decade. From 1973, when the Arab oil embargo began, until the collapse of worldwide oil prices in 1986, the U.S. consumption of energy hardly grew at all—even though economic output climbed 40 percent. Since then, energy use had risen slightly faster than economic growth. This turn of events was attributed mainly to lower petroleum prices, which made American motorists less interested in fuel economy. It also reflected the Reagan administration's energy policies.

Energy-Policy Questions

Among the energy-policy questions facing President Bush and his secretary of energy, James D. Watkins, were these:

• Should the decline in U.S. oil production be allowed to continue, or should the government take steps to reverse it?

• Should the nation be encouraged to switch from oil to other energy sources?

• Should the decline in the nuclear-energy and uranium industries be allowed to continue?

• Should the opening of the monopolistic natural-gas and electric-utility markets proposed by the Reagan administration go forward or be stopped?

• Should the United States be ready with the energy technologies needed for the decades and centuries ahead, if, as some predicted, fossil fuels became too harmful or too scarce to burn?

• How should the nation avoid the kind of devastating economic pain that resulted from the failure of U.S. industry and government to foresee and prepare for the oil shocks of the 1970s?

To the oil industry, the paramount concern was how to increase production and profits. To the consumer, it was how to lower heating-oil and gasoline prices, and ensure reliable supplies. To the environmentalist, it was how to avoid pollution of the land and sea in extracting and transporting the oil.

The problem most likely to impress those in the White House was that of "national security" —such as was raised by the oil embargo, when several of the world's big oil producers refused to sell their oil to American markets because of U.S. support of Israel in the 1973 Arab-Israeli war. Few of the lessons learned from that experience had really stuck. Lower prices and greater availability—as more oil fields were tapped outside the Middle East—tended to make Americans forget the long lines at the gas stations, and to erase the thought that eventually the world would run out of cheap oil.

By 1989 the United States had used up most of its cheap oil, and what remained was increasingly costly to produce. To obtain cheap oil, this country had to turn to foreign markets. As the demand grew, the United States was steadily importing more and more oil. However, America depended far less than it did in the 1970s on oil from the Organization of Petroleum Exporting Countries (OPEC), whose cartel arrangement sent world prices soaring after the embargo. Faced with increased competition from other countries where discoveries were being made, the cartel fell into disarray. The United States developed new sources of supply elsewhere, especially in the Western Hemisphere. It also created a Strategic Petroleum Reserve, an underground storage of oil for emergency use.

The oil industry called for government action to boost domestic production of oil by leasing the last big government-owned reserves in wildlife refuges and offshore tracts, and giving tax breaks. Conservationists claimed this approach would "drain America first," and thus hurt rather then help energy security. Bush indicated in his fiscal 1990 budget he sided with the oil industry. He proposed four tax breaks, costing the government $300 million in 1990, as incentives for oil and gas drillers.

Several proposals in recent years for an import fee on oil and for a higher tax on gasoline at the pump had failed to attract substantial support in Congress. The import fee had been advocated as a means of aiding the domestic industry by pushing up the price of imported oil. Both the fee and the higher pump tax were seen as ways of reducing the growing American appetite for gasoline and thus reducing the U.S. foreign trade deficit.

At confirmation hearings before the Senate Energy Committee, Watkins offered little hope that the president would relent in his opposition to an oil-import fee. And a higher gasoline tax would run counter to the president's promise of no new taxes.

Watkins did say that he would try to forge an "integrated energy strategy" to reduce dependence on oil imports. He spoke of the need for an energy policy built on a wide range of sources in "a sensible economic mixture." He said that achieving a technology for burning coal cleanly was "one of my greatest personal interests." Watkins also said he would be "an advocate" for solar and renewable energy programs that were cut back in Bush's 1990 budget.

Nuclear Power's Future?

The decisions that the president and his energy secretary would make would do much to determine whether commercial nuclear power shriveled and died or was reborn. Safety problems, cost overruns, shoddy construction, regulatory delays, slow growth of electric demand, and other factors had halted the nation's investment in nuclear power in the 1980s. Utilities had ordered no new commercial nuclear reactors since 1978. Nuclear plants produced only about 17 percent of the nation's electric power. That amount would increase somewhat because the construction of some plants ordered before 1978 was still under way. Others, however, had been abandoned.

Accidents at Three Mile Island, Pennsylvania, in 1979 and Chernobyl, the Soviet Union, in 1986 raised worldwide concern about the safety of nuclear facilities. In the 100th Congress, however, the nuclear industry did comparatively well, winning renewal of the Price-Anderson Act, which limits the industry's liability in the event of a plant disaster that results in widespread damage or death.

In addition to public fears of deadly radiation being accidentally released into the countryside, such as at Chernobyl, the nuclear industry had been haunted by the problem of how to store radioactive waste material.

Safety questions also arose over the storage of wastes from the government's own nuclear-weapons production program. Pollution and safety woes had afflicted the weapons reactors that the Department of Energy operates for the Department of Defense. Most warheads had to be regularly recharged with the tritium these reactors produced, or they would lose their potency. But due to safety concerns, all the reactors that produced the tritium were shut down. Still other plants had serious pollution problems caused by their methods of hazardous waste disposal.

Some environmental groups had sued to keep the plants closed until these problems were addressed. Advocates of a strong military, on the other hand, worried that national security could be weakened if production was not restarted soon, and were pushing for construction of new weapons plants. In accepting his nomination as energy secretary, Watkins emphasized "my longstanding conviction that environmental and energy objectives can be made mutually compatible.... I reject the stamp of mutual exclusivity that some would arbitrarily assign to them."

At his confirmation hearing, Watkins—a retired admiral with long experience in nuclear power and weaponry—said he would shake up the program's management to ensure safety. All reactors capable of producing material needed to recharge U.S. nuclear warheads were then shut down for safety reasons. The ultimate cleanup cost had been estimated to run more than $100 billion—a potentially budget-wrecking sum that would necessarily be spread over many years.

On February 21, 1989, at another congressional hearing, Rep. John M. Spratt, Jr., D-S.C., released a plan that had been drafted by the Department of Energy for modernizing the nuclear-weapons-production system by the year 2010. The plan had been suppressed by the Reagan administration, Spratt said, because it did not conform to Reagan's budget policy. The plan indicated that funding for new plant construction would grow rapidly over the next five years. For modernization and cleanup in fiscal 1990, Bush asked Congress for outlays of $3.2 billion—a billion more than Reagan had requested and $700 million more than was approved for 1989.

Other items on the nuclear-industry shopping list of legislation were a reorganization of the Nuclear Regulatory Commission; streamlined, one-step licensing; and standardized reactor design. The uranium industry, which supplies much of the fuel used in nuclear-power plants, wanted import protection.

The idea of a nuclear renaissance did not seem far-fetched to many in the industry. One key would be development of new reactor technologies inherently much safer than existing reactors. Industry leaders also hoped smaller, modular designs would reduce financial risk to utilities. They likewise stressed that nuclear power offered reduced dependence on the use of environmentally troubling fossil fuels. Unfortunately, it would raise major environmental disadvantages of its own. In addition to the problem of nuclear waste, the nuclear industry would ask the government to expand funding for research on future reactors. But anti-nuclear groups would argue that the industry was large and profitable enough to fund its own research.

The real security threat, said conservationists from both parties in Congress, would come from an inability to switch from one fuel to another in response to changing market conditions. Even as companies fretted about oil and national security during the last several years, the nation had such a glut of unused natural gas that low prices were hurting producers.

Gas had replaced oil in many jobs, and was so cheap that it was competing with coal as a power-plant fuel. It had the advantage of being cleaner than either coal or oil. Federal laws and Federal Energy Regulatory Commission rules restricted markets by allowing major gas-pipeline and electric-power companies to limit other companies' access to interstate facilities. That meant consumers didn't always get energy from the sources that produced it most cheaply.

11

A 'Drug Czar' Maps Strategy

The Bush administration added the country's first "drug czar," a position authorized by Congress in 1988 anti-drug-legislation, in an attempt to coordinate the federal government's various activities to deal with the nation's rising drug problem. That law set aside $3.5 million for the new Office of National Drug Control Policy and ordered the director to develop a drug-control strategy within six months of taking office.

To that office, which was accorded cabinet-level status, President Bush named William J. Bennett, who had been President Reagan's outspoken secretary of education. Upon taking position, Bennett was introduced by Bush at a White House press conference on February 8, 1989, as a man "with a million ideas" —which the president suggested he would need because "the law is very unclear on how we use his imagination and ability to bring together all agencies of this government in this fight."

Confirmation hearings were held before the Senate Judiciary Committee. Chairman Joseph R. Biden, Jr., D-Del.— the new law's principal architect—said the drug czar should begin by making an independent analysis of the drug problem, then seek the views of the heads of government agencies, members of Congress, and experts outside of government. Biden said the direc-

tor should next submit a detailed, specific strategy to the president.

After the president approved a plan, Biden said, the affected agencies could submit budgets to the director of the Office of National Drug Control Policy and to the Office of Management and Budget. The director would certify requests and draft a consolidated budget. Any differences between OMB and the drug control office would be resolved by the president. Congress would review the strategy and budget priorities. "We will be able for the first time to hold some accountable," Biden added. The position was created, he said, to end "petty, jurisdictional" conflicts among drug-fighting agencies.

Bennett:
An Outspoken Iconoclast

Bush's selection of Bennett was expected to keep the government's drug fight front and center. As secretary of education in 1985-88, Bennett had used the office as his own "bully pulpit" to expose what he considered to be the ills of the country's education system. Bennett had made his mark not only for what he said, but also for how he said it.

For example, five days after taking office in February 1985, Bennett attacked the student loan program, saying that proposed cuts would lead to healthy "divestiture of some sorts—stereo divestiture, automobile divestiture, three-weeks-at-the-beach divestiture."

He attacked colleges for "greed" in raising tuition twice as fast as inflation; he accused trade schools of recruiting ill-prepared students just to get those students' federal-aid stipends; and he regularly accused teachers' unions of blocking needed reforms in public education. Bennett's parting shot, when he announced in May 1988 that he would leave office, was a declaration that "the department's not necessary."

Although Bennett offered no direct experience in drug enforcement, as secretary of education he regularly had called for more forceful anti-drug policies and more resources for the fight. Sen. Dennis DeConcini, D-Ariz., one of the authors of the drug law, turned down the job nine days before Bush announced Bennett's appointment on January 12. Both DeConcini and Biden expressed concern about Bennett's lack of drug-enforcement experience.

However, on March 9, Bennett passed quietly through the confirmation process and was approved by the Senate on a 97-2 vote. Earlier that day, the Senate Judiciary Committee had approved the nomination 13-1. Paul Simon, D-Ill., cast the lone committee vote against Bennett. On the floor vote, he and Sen. Jeff Bingaman, D-N.M., cast the only Senate "no" votes. Both criticized Bennett's leadership as secretary of education.

The goal of a national drug strategy, Bennett said during his confirmation hearings, "is a steady reduction in the flow of drugs through our streets and communities, and a corresponding reduction in the deadly hold they now have over so many of our friends and families and neighbors." He would not specify what strategies he would

Office of National Drug Policy

William J. Bennett

use until he had studied the situation.

Nevertheless, he was not long in making his views known on one subject. On March 14, at Bennett's urging, the Bush administration suspended the importation of semiautomatic assault weapons, such as the AK-47 rifle. Just recently, a gunman had used such a weapon to kill five children and wound thirty others in a schoolyard at Stockton, California; assault rifles also were known to be favored weapons of drug dealers. (Once the import ban was announced, Colt Industries, the American gun manufacturer, promptly announced it was voluntarily suspending commercial sales of its AR-15 rifle.)

Bush, a member of the National Rifle Association, had on several occasions opposed gun controls. However, he said at a White House news conference March 7, "I do think that there has to be some assurance that these automated attack weapons are not used in the manner they're being used." He asked Bennett to study the problem, and the new director of drug-control policy lost no time. The director cited a rising tide of drug-related violence, especially in urban areas.

Then, on April 10, Bennett unveiled an "emergency" plan to increase federal law-enforcement activity against the District of Columbia's scourge of drugs and crime. By the end of summer, he said, he would have a nationwide strategy for combating illegal drugs. In the meantime, the drug czar said that he would have an opportunity to see what worked, and what did not, in his own backyard.

Almost immediately, part of his local plan went awry—indicating that inter-agency coordination had some glitches. He spoke of adding two prisons for criminals in the nation's capital, but later his aides said there was no need for one of the prisons because of a federal prison being built in Maryland.

Bennett also spoke of new "pilot" programs of drug rehabilitation, and efforts by the Department of Housing and Urban Development to drive out drug pushers from federally supported housing projects. The *New York Times* commented editorially that the success of the plan "may eventually turn on how the new interagency task force shapes up." The newspaper added, "the exercise makes clear that for a truly determined effort, there is only one czar, George Bush."

12

The Cabinet

George Bush, the consummate Washington insider, turned to familiar figures with government experience to fill most of the cabinet-level positions in his new administration. His campaign vow to bring "fresh faces" to the nation's capital was honored only occasionally in making his choices. There were press references to his "Beltway team," using a political metaphor that derives from a highway encircling the city.

Like Bush, many of his appointees arose from the institutions of education, business, and government, collectively known as the Eastern establishment. They were the kind of insiders Ronald Reagan—and Jimmy Carter before him—came to Washington to vanquish. William A. Niskanen, a former Reagan adviser, said Bush's cabinet was "an extraordinarily competent group." But, he added, "it's competence without a compass. These are people who have accepted the dimensions of the modern state." In that regard the Bush administration, while in one sense a continuation of Reagan's, might have more in common with the Nixon-Ford administrations in which Bush also served.

Although Bush began naming his key people the day after the election, the upper echelons of several departments and agencies remained sparsely staffed two months after he took office. For instance, the *Wall* *Street Journal* reported at the end of February that Sen. Christopher J. Dodd, D-Conn., tried to call the State Department to discuss Central America and, to his surprise, Secretary of State James A. Baker III himself answered the phone. The reason, the paper said, was that the Bush administration was slow to fill the department's positions, and "there wasn't anyone else who could have a substantive discussion with the senator."

Other press criticisms claimed that the Bush team was slow in taking control, and thus losing an opportunity to move ahead with legislative programs at a time when Congress tended to be most receptive to a new president.

Bush stoutly denied that his administration lacked direction, as was suggested repeatedly in questions at a White House news conference March 7. However, the honeymoon period that a new president traditionally enjoys with the legislative branch was cut short by the Senate's rejection of Bush's first nominee for secretary of defense, John Tower, a Republican former senator from Texas. The defeat marked only the ninth time in two centuries that a president had been refused his cabinet choice, and it was the first time that the refusal had come at the beginning of an administration. The last previous rejection occurred in 1959, toward the close of Dwight D. Eisenhower's second term, when the Senate voted down his nomination of Lewis L. Strauss as secretary of commerce.

By a 47-53 vote on March 9, 1989, the Senate refused to confirm Tower's appointment after often-heated debate between Democratic and Republican senators over their former colleague's fitness for the defense post. With but four exceptions, the vote was along party lines. Only one Republican, Nancy Landon Kassebaum of Kansas, voted against Tower and only three Democrats—Lloyd Bentsen of Texas, Christopher J. Dodd of Connecticut, and Howell Heflin of Alabama—voted for him.

The Democrats' fight against Tower's confirmation was led by Sam Nunn of Georgia, chairman of the Senate Armed Services Committee, a position that Tower had held from 1981 until he retired from the Senate in 1984. At issue were Tower's drinking habits and his consulting work with the defense industry after he left the Senate. The debate focused on confidential FBI summaries of more than four hundred interviews with persons who knew Tower. Such reports are routinely submitted on behalf of all nominees, but they usually receive little public attention.

In this instance, Nunn and several of his Democratic colleagues said they found a record of alcohol abuse that made Tower an unwise choice to put next in line to the president in the chain of military command. Moreover, they contended that his lucrative consulting contracts with weapons makers would impair his ability to restore public trust to a scandal-plagued Pentagon weapons-buying system. Republicans, in nearly equal numbers, said Tower's critics relied on unfounded allegations by anonymous sources. They concluded that the FBI reports did not render Tower unfit for the job, and they accused the Democrats of creating an issue purposely to embarrass and possibly weaken the new president.

Democrats denied that this was their motive and pointed out that they had readily endorsed Bush's other top nominees. In fact, they joined with Senate Republicans in unanimously voting (92-0) to confirm the president's selection of Rep. Dick Cheney for the defense position once Tower was rejected. Cheney, Wyoming's at-large representative, was starting his sixth term in the House and had recently been elected its minority whip, the No. 2 Republican leadership post in that body. He had previously served in the White House under Presidents Richard Nixon and Gerald Ford, becoming Ford's chief of staff during his last year in office.

In contrast to the long fight over Tower, Cheney was confirmed quickly, after only one public hearing. That hearing by the Senate Armed Services Committee, was a clubby conclave. The senators bandied inside jokes as they applauded the elevation of a respected colleague. Cheney lacked Tower's standing as a former leader among Republicans in congressional defense debates. But as a senior Republican on the House Intelligence subcommittee on budgetary oversight, Cheney told the committee that he had followed intelligence and strategic arms programs. His immediate priority, he said, was filling some forty civilian policy positions at the Pentagon.

Cheney was the last of the cabinet-level appointees, although several positions just below that level were still unfilled by April 1989. On the same day the Senate approved Cheney, March 17, it also confirmed Lawrence S. Eagleburger, a retired foreign service officer, to be deputy secretary of state, the No. 2 position in the State Department.

One of Bush's very first acts after his election was to name Baker, his campaign manager, secretary of state. Baker, who had been Ronald Reagan's White House chief of staff and secretary of the treasury, encountered no difficulty winning Senate con-

Bush's Views on Judicial Appointments

In discussing the judicial appointments he would be called on to make, George Bush had used Ronald Reagan's rhetoric. But Bush was not Reagan, and his inner circle was not dominated by Reagan's hard-line conservatives.

Bush had said that he wanted judges who would "not legislate from the bench, who will interpret the Constitution." And he said he had no litmus test for nominees—that his nominees would not be required to hold a favored position on, say, abortion or busing.

All that would seem unobjectionable to both Democrats and Republicans, except for the political coloring phrases such as "legislate from the bench" or "judicial activism" took on in the Nixon and Reagan presidencies. As the judicial-appointments debate was framed by conservatives, such phrases suggested a judge who substitutes his beliefs for the intent of the legislators who wrote the law. Judicial activism might be a trial judge's decision to take over the operation of a school system in response to complaints about racial discrimination. "Judicial restraint," in contrast, had come to describe a judge's deference to legislative intent or reluctance to go beyond the explicit words of the Constitution.

These political notions would likely be widely aired if Bush had to fill one or more Supreme Court vacancies, as was highly probable. Three of the justices on the liberal wing of the court—William J. Brennan, Jr., Thurgood Marshall, and Harry A. Blackmun—were eighty or older. In addition, when Bush took office he had about thirty judgeships to fill on federal district and appellate courts.

Democrats and Republicans on the Senate Judiciary Committee predicted that the nomination process would be more open with Bush. Orrin G. Hatch, R-Utah, a senior member, expected key members of the committee "to be consulted on a wide variety of appointments."

In their 1987 rejection of Robert H. Bork for the Supreme Court, Senate Democrats put the Reagan White House on notice that the judicial philosophy of high-court nominees would not escape close examination in the confirmation process. Bork, hailed by his supporters as a brilliant jurist but labeled by critics as a rigid, conservative ideologue, came under intense questioning about his legal views and judicial bent. Anthony M. Kennedy underwent similar questioning before the Senate confirmed him early in 1988. Kennedy assumed a more conservative stance on the court than many people had expected. Thus the positions that justices take can surprise the senators who approve them, no less than the presidents who appoint them.

firmation. In separate unanimous votes of 99-0 on January 25, the Senate confirmed Baker, and also Elizabeth H. Dole as secretary of labor. Dole, the only woman selected for Bush's cabinet, had been Reagan's secretary of transportation until she resigned in 1987 to assist her husband, Senate Republican leader Robert Dole, in his race against

Bush for the party's presidential nomination.

In another job-swap, Clayton K. Yeutter, U.S. trade representative for Reagan, became secretary of agriculture.

Three members of Bush's cabinet retained the the same posts they had held in Reagan's final cabinet and did not require confirmation again. They were Nicholas F. Brady, who had replaced Baker as secretary of the treasury, Secretary of Education Lauro F. Cavazos, and Attorney General Dick Thornburgh. Still other familiar faces returned. Bush named William J. Bennett, Cavazos's outspoken predecessor, to the newly created post of "drug czar," and James D. Watkins as secretary of energy. Although Watkins, a retired admiral, had not held political office before, he had served in Washington as chief of naval operations and, upon his retirement from uniform, as director of Reagan's special commission on AIDS (Acquired Immune Deficiency Syndrome).

Besides Cheney, who was a member of Congress when nominated, Bush recruited three former House Republicans for his cabinet: Jack F. Kemp, of New York, to run the Department of Housing and Urban Development (HUD); Manuel Lujan, Jr., of New Mexico, to run the Department of the Interior; and Edward J. Derwinski, of Illinois, to run the newly created Department of Veterans Affairs. Kemp, like Robert Dole, was a rival of Bush for the presidential nomination. Neither he nor Lujan sought reelection to Congress in 1986. Derwinski was defeated for reelection in 1982 and then held high-level positions in the State Department.

As for cabinet "outsiders," Bush named Samuel K. Skinner secretary of transportation, and Dr. Louis W. Sullivan secretary of Health and Human Services (HHS). Skinner had been chairman of the Regional Transportation Authority of Northeastern Illinois. Sullivan, a physician,

was the founder and president of the Morehouse School of Medicine in Atlanta. Bush's choice for secretary of commerce was a longtime friend, Robert A. Mosbacher, a Texas oil millionaire. As the chief fund raiser in Bush's 1980 and 1988 presidential campaigns, Mosbacher could hardly be considered a political outsider even though he could not claim long government experience in Washington.

Of all the nominees, Sullivan was the only one other than Tower who encountered any real difficulty in the nomination process. Unlike Tower, Sullivan's problem was short-lived and he won the Senate's approval.

James A. Baker III
Secretary of State

Within hours of his election victory, Bush designated his close associate, James A. Baker III, as secretary of state. He and Bush had been hunting, fishing, and tennis buddies for more than two decades, and he ran Bush's presidential campaigns in 1980 and 1988. Moreover, Baker was White House chief of staff in President Reagan's first term and secretary of the treasury in Reagan's second.

Baker enjoyed tremendous prestige— at least in that part of Washington's establishment where "pragmatist" was not a dirty word—as a canny political operative, more inclined toward negotiation than confrontation in dealing with Congress and foreign governments. Typical of that viewpoint, House Majority Leader Thomas S. Foley, D-Wash., lauded the choice of Baker as "an excellent appointment. . . . He has wide respect on both sides of the Hill." Sen. J. Bennett Johnston, D-La., called Baker "one of the smoothest operators around, and I say that in a good sense."

Baker's reputation for political savvy rested in part on his track record in the executive branch where, as a manager, he was skilled at ranking issues according to their importance and concentrating on those with the highest priority. Another aspect of Baker's image is that of a persistent but congenial negotiator. In his various roles, he handled personally lengthy and complex discussions with congressional Democrats over tax policy, and with foreign governments over trade and currency issues. One of his first deeds in the new Bush administration was to work out a compromise between Congress and the White House on aid for Nicaraguan contras.

However, a minority viewpoint that was more skeptical of Baker's much-touted pragmatism existed. Some of these critics were self-styled "movement conservatives" who complained that, in his eagerness to strike deals with congressional Democrats, Baker compromised elements of the Reagan program. In the October 17, 1988, issue of the *New Republic,* columnist Fred Barnes attacked Baker's reputation from a different direction. In concentrating on doing the "doable," Barnes suggested, Baker had dodged some of the toughest problems, such as the soaring federal deficit.

Conspicuously absent from Baker's résumé was any direct experience in U.S.-Soviet relations or other traditional major foreign policy issues. But that was offset by two factors. First, Bush, whose own résumé included the posts of ambassador to the United Nations and to China, and director of the CIA, had considerable experience in foreign and national security policy. Second, economic issues had assumed a growing importance in the international arena. The expanding agenda of foreign policy matters confronting the secretary of state included two issues on which Baker spent much of his time at Treasury:

● How to alleviate the economic burden borne by developing countries with huge debts to foreign lenders.

● How to stabilize the relationships among nations' currencies and thus rational-

James A. Baker III

Ken Heinen

Born to wealthy Houston family on April 28, 1930 . . . graduated from Princeton University and the University of Texas law school, with two years out for Marine Corps . . . entered politics in 1970, running Bush's losing Senate campaign . . . under secretary of commerce in Ford administration . . . campaign manager for Ford in 1976 and for Reagan in 1980 . . . with second wife, has combined family of eight children.

ize international trading patterns.

Baker is in the fourth generation of a family of wealthy Houston lawyers. He studied the classics at Princeton and served two years in the Marine Corps before returning to his home state to take his law degree at the University of Texas. When his first wife died of cancer in 1970, Baker threw himself into the unsuccessful Senate campaign of his close friend, George Bush.

In 1975 Bush landed him a job as undersecretary of commerce, and in 1976 Baker managed President Gerald Ford's unsuccessful election campaign. In 1978 Baker launched his own bid for office, running for attorney general of Texas. His campaign assumed the Democratic nominee would be a liberal, Price Daniel, Jr. But the Democrats selected the more conservative Mark White, who handily defeated Baker and went on to win the Texas governorship in 1980.

Baker also managed Bush's 1980 bid for the Republican nomination for president, an effort in which his characteristic pragmatism ultimately disturbed some Bush supporters. When Reagan clearly began pulling ahead, Baker pushed Bush to withdraw from the race. He later justified the move as essential to giving Bush a shot at the second spot on the 1980 GOP ticket.

Baker's pragmatism paid off for both men, of course; Bush went on the ticket, and Baker managed the triumphant presidential campaign that fall. It was during that period that the campaign obtained confidential material from the reelection campaign of President Jimmy Carter. In 1983 the FBI questioned Baker about the acquisition of the illicit material, but he disclaimed any knowledge, and the investigation came to nothing.

In November 1980 Baker was named Reagan's chief of staff, becoming one of a triumvirate that would run the White House. The other two were longtime Reagan retainers Edwin Meese III, who was given the title of counselor to the president, and Michael K. Deaver, who became deputy chief of staff. GOP conservatives, suspicious of Baker's loyalty because of his opposition to Reagan in 1976 and 1980, were assured that the conservative Meese would handle the making of policy; Baker, they were told, would oversee its execution.

But the distinction between policy making and administration proved as spurious as ever: By the end of 1981, the disciplined Baker had assumed strong influence over the policy formulation process nominally run by the relatively disorganized Meese. Conservatives bewailed Baker's apostasy from the "true" Reagan agenda when he joined budget chief David A. Stockman to support a tax increase as part of a budget compromise with Congress in 1982.

In 1985 upon becoming secretary of the treasury, Baker was again charged with betraying conservative goals when he plunged into negotiations with Democrats to bring about a compromise tax-overhaul bill. In his three years at Treasury, Baker evidently succeeded in guiding the dollar through a controlled devaluation relative to other currencies in order to bolster economic growth at home and reduce the trade deficit. To do that, he had first to overturn the administration's strong ideological opposition to government intervention in currency markets.

Baker was less successful in his efforts to deal with Third World debt. In 1985 he introduced the "Baker plan" to world financial leaders, proposing that commercial banks make even greater lending to many of the heavily indebted Third World countries to stimulate their economies and encourage them to open up their markets to international trade. The banks resisted, and little came of his effort.

Nicholas F. Brady
Secretary of the Treasury

For his second cabinet selection, Bush asked his longtime confidant Nicholas F. Brady to stay on as secretary of the treasury. President Reagan named Brady to that post the previous August when Baker left to run Bush's presidential campaign. Bush emphasized that Brady—who had spent a career on Wall Street with periodic, short-term stints in public service—would serve as the administration's economic spokesman.

Brady had served briefly as a Republican senator from New Jersey, filling the unexpired term of Sen. Harrison A. Williams, Jr., in 1982. But he was probably best known to the public as the chairman of the so-called Brady commission, formally the Presidential Task Force on Market Mechanisms. After the October 1987 stock market crash, President Reagan picked Brady and four other prominent businessmen to investigate the causes of the crash and recommend ways to prevent a recurrence.

The commission's report was the first of five similar studies issued in 1988 and was probably the most important. Its central recommendation, to bring various markets under centralized and stronger regulatory control, drew praise but little action in Congress. It also drew a critical response from Wall Street, and some hostility from the White House. The government was torn by conflicting advice on what steps to take, and it ended up making few changes in the present system of regulating the markets. Nevertheless, Brady's appointment to the Treasury was well received in Washington. He drew few hard questions at his confirmation hearing and won Senate approval on September 14, 1988, by a vote of 92-2. Brady warmly embraced the Reagan administration's economic policies. He defended Bush's promise not to raise taxes and offered the view that little more needed to be done to ensure future stability of the world's securities markets. As for the federal budget deficit, he adopted Bush's view that the country could "grow its way" out of the deficit with a healthy economy.

Brady generally maintained a low profile during his first months at Treasury. However, he did seize on one issue: the growing financial crisis that faced the savings and loan industry and its deposit-insur-

Nicholas F. Brady

AP

Born to wealthy New York City family on April 11, 1930 ... graduated from Yale and Harvard, with a master's degree in business administration ... joined investment firm of Dillon, Read & Co. immediately after graduating ... became chairman and chief executive officer, 1982 ... filled unexpired term of Sen. Harrison A. Williams, Jr., D-N.J., in 1982 ... chaired the Presidential Task Force on Market Mechanisms that examined the October 1987 stock market crash ... appointed secretary of the treasury by President Reagan August 5, 1988 ... married, with four children; home at Far Hills, New Jersey.

ance fund. Brady ordered a Treasury study of the problem, and he became the chief draftsman of the bailout plan, which was Bush's first big legislative initiative after taking office.

Brady also put the United States on a new course toward reducing the Third World debt burden. Breaking with Reagan

Lauro F. Cavazos

Department of Education

Born January 4, 1927, the son of a King Ranch cattle foreman in Kingsville, Texas ... served in the U.S. Army at the end of World War II ... graduated from Texas Tech University in 1951 with a bachelor's degree in zoology and a master's in cytology ... earned a Ph.D. in physiology from Iowa State University in 1954 ... taught anatomy at the Medical College of Virginia and Tufts University ... became a dean at Tufts and, in 1980, president of Texas Tech ... was nominated for education secretary by President Reagan August 9, 1988, and confirmed by the Senate in September, becoming the first Hispanic cabinet member ... married, with ten children

administration policy, Brady indicated that the United States would begin to urge "debt reduction." This signified an effort to use the financial resources of the industrialized nations to encourage commercial banks to write down some of their loans to the Third World.

Lauro F. Cavazos
Secretary of Education

Lauro F. Cavazos became the first Hispanic cabinet member when he was tapped by Reagan in August 1988 to replace William J. Bennett. The nomination won warm praise from educators and Hispanic groups, although some speculated that it was a political ploy to woo Hispanics and win Bush support from Texas, the new cabinet member's home state.

Cavazos was then president of Texas Tech University in Lubbock, not far from the west Texas country where he grew up. He served in World War II and received a bachelor's and then a master's degree at Texas Tech. He went on to earn a doctorate at Iowa State University in physiology, and afterward taught anatomy at the Medical College of Virginia and Tufts University, before returning to his alma mater in 1980 as its president.

His nomination sailed through the Senate, propelled by a promise to try to boost federal funding for education. The Senate unanimously confirmed Cavazos September 20, 1988.

Unlike Bennett, Cavazos kept a low profile as secretary of education. He has sought to win the support of the same educators that Bennett often blasted. This approach, while generally lauded by educators, might undermine attempts by Cavazos to focus the nation's attention on education. Bennett made enemies, but his attack-dog style also drew headlines and heightened public interest in the education system's shortcomings.

Dick Cheney
Secretary of Defense

As secretary of defense, Dick Cheney must work closely with Congress, where he spent the previous ten years and rose rapidly to leadership positions. Shortly before President Bush named him to the defense post, his fellow House Republicans chose him whip, the party's No. 2 leadership position in that chamber. His ascent in the House was attributed to a conservative voting record and a close alliance with moderate Republican leader Robert H. Michel of Illinois.

Cheney was White House chief of staff under President Gerald R. Ford before winning Wyoming's sole House seat in 1978. After just two years in the chamber, he became chairman of the Republican Policy Committee and made it a vehicle for his upward movement. He actively supported Michel's 1980 bid for minority leader and moved up in 1987, unchallenged, to chairman of the House Republican Conference.

In 1987, as the senior Republican on the House Select Committee investigating the Iran-contra affair, Cheney was one of the most impassioned defenders of Reagan's support of armed contras trying to overthrow the Sandinista government in Nicaragua. Nevertheless, he worked closely with Rep. Lee H. Hamilton, D-Ind., the committee chairman, to minimize partisan disputes over the committee's operations.

Though staunchly partisan, Cheney reveled in his independence. He was part of a Republican revolt against Reagan's tax-overhaul bill in 1985. Even after the president patched things up with other Republicans, Cheney stood pat in his opposition, saying the tax bill was "bad legislation."

As a member of the House Interior and Insular Affairs Committee, he stood firm for the cattle industry's interests and helped prodevelopment forces win some concessions from the committee's environmentally

Dick Cheney

Lisa Berg

Born in Lincoln, Nebraska, January 20, 1941 ... reared in Casper, Wyoming ... University of Wyoming, A.B. 1965, M.A. 1966, and postgraduate studies at the University of Wisconsin, 1966-68 ... served on staff of Rep. William A. Steiger, R-Wis., as a congressional fellow, 1969; special assistant to director of antipoverty agency, 1969-70, and White House post of deputy to the president's counsellor, 1971-73 ... assistant director Cost of Living Council, 1971-73 ... financial consultant to private company, 1973-74 ... deputy to White House chief of staff Donald Rumsfeld in 1974-75 ... chief of staff, 1975-77 ... elected to Congress from Wyoming's at-large district in 1978 and reelected five times ... married, with two children.

minded majority. But during his ten years in Congress, Cheney was often more closely identified with foreign policy than the regional issues usually uppermost in the minds of western lawmakers. He complained on several occasions that Congress was hampering the president's ability to carry out foreign policy.

Although Cheney grew up in Wyoming, his political career began in Washington, where he had spent much of his adult life. As a political science graduate student at the University of Wisconsin, Cheney came to the nation's capital in 1967 on a congressional fellowship. He stayed to take a job under Donald J. Rumsfeld at the Office of Economic Opportunity, the antipoverty agency and followed Rumsfeld to the White House in 1971. When Ford succeeded Richard Nixon, Rumsfeld became Ford's chief of staff. The next year, 1975, the job was passed on to Cheney when Rumsfeld became secretary of defense.

Cheney shared some of Rumsfeld's moderate Republican reputation during those years but appeared more conservative in Congress. He voted Wyoming's antigovernment sentiments, but negotiated with the other side on a friendly basis. He became a member of the House Intelligence Committee in 1985, where he was an advocate of U.S. military spending.

Cheney's lack of military service was no barrier to Congress's approval of his defense appointment. He was of draft age during the Vietnam War but had a "sole provider" deferment because he was married in 1964, the year he received his undergraduate degree from the University of Wyoming. In announcing Cheney's appointment, Bush said: "He's a thoughtful man, a quiet man, a strong man, [and] approaches public policy with vigor, determination, and diligence."

Edward J. Derwinski
Secretary of Veterans Affairs

For all the news leaks about Bush's cabinet appointments, Edward J. Derwin-

Edward J. Derwinski

Born in Chicago September 15, 1926 . . . graduated from Loyola University . . . served in U.S. Army during World War II . . . representative to Illinois General Assembly, 1957-58 . . . member of U.S. House of Representatives, 1959-83 . . . ranking Republican on Post Office and Civil Service Committee and second ranking on Foreign Affairs Committee . . . served in State Department 1983-88, most recently as under secretary for security assistance, science, and technology . . . member of American Legion, Amvets, Catholic War Veterans, Polish Legion of American Veterans, and Veterans of Foreign Wars . . . married, with two children.

ski's name seemed to be on nobody's lips when he was tapped to be the nation's first secretary of veterans affairs. In 1988 Congress voted to elevate the Veterans Administration to cabinet status, effective the following March 15.

In nominating Derwinski, Bush reached out to a longtime friend. The two had served together in the House of Representatives in the late 1960s, when Derwinski was already a "somewhat senior member of Congress" and Bush was just a "young, innocent freshman," the nominee recalled. Derwinski fitted into Bush's pattern of picking fairly moderate conservatives for top positions in his administration.

When Derwinski was first elected to Congress in 1958, he was a right-winger with rather narrow ideas. But during his twenty-four-year tenure, he became more mainstream and gained a reputation for working with members in both political parties. In 1982 Derwinski lost his congressional seat in the Republican primary to a fellow incumbent in a suburban Chicago district that had been merged with Derwinski's. After leaving Congress, he spent the next six years in upper-echelon positions in the State Department.

During his years in Congress, he also became an expert on both foreign affairs issues and problems facing the country's federal workers. Veterans' groups anticipate that his familiarity with the way the civil service operates, as well as his own experiences in the Army in World War II, would help him identify with the needs of veterans.

John Hanson, deputy director of public relations for the American Legion, described Derwinski as a "pleasant, knowledgeable guy." However, John Wanamaker, deputy director of legislative affairs for the Retired Officers Association, said: "In veterans' circles, he hasn't made much of a mark one way or another."

Derwinski faced a challenge unlike that of any other cabinet secretary. He was placed in charge of carrying out a new law requiring the old Veterans Administration

to be upgraded and turned into a cabinet-level department by March 15, 1989. In other areas, he would fight the same battles as his peers—namely, protecting funds from budget cuts. Many VA hospitals, short on staff, needed a cash infusion to remain open. And as veterans from World War II and the Korean War grew older, other health costs were expected to rise greatly.

Derwinski promised in a Senate confirmation hearing March 2 "to make the cause of the VA budget my cause." But he confirmed that he had made comments to the American Legion a few days earlier that, given fiscal realities, veterans would not be the Bush administration's "priority group." The Senate Veterans Affairs Committee unanimously recommended his confirmation, which the Senate endorsed on a vote of 94-0.

Elizabeth H. Dole
Secretary of Labor

In picking Elizabeth H. Dole for his secretary of labor, Bush not only chose one of official Washington's most popular figures, he made conciliatory gestures toward past and potential adversaries. Her selection met with general approval from members of both parties in Congress, and from both business and organized labor, despite the mixed record that Dole left as Reagan's transportation secretary for more than four years.

In a brief press conference, neither Bush nor Dole offered details of the incoming administration's policies on a number of controversial labor issues that would test its relations with Congress and special-interest groups. Without offering specifics, Bush and Dole said they had discussed the need for job training, workplace safety, "more public-private partnerships," and protection of workers' rights. Dole did say that Bush's proposal to give a tax credit for child care "is a very good one because it provides choice for families."

Democrats and labor leaders harbored

Elizabeth H. Dole

Teresa Zabala

Born in Salisbury, North Carolina, July 29, 1936 . . . graduated from Duke University in 1958, Phi Beta Kappa, with political science major . . . Harvard University, master's degree in education, 1960, and law degree, 1965 . . . staff assistant, Department of Health, Education, and Welfare, 1966-67 . . . in private law practice, 1967-68 . . . Presidential Commission for Consumer Interests, 1968-71 . . . deputy director, Office of Consumer Affairs, 1971-73 . . . Nixon appointee to Federal Trade Commission, 1973-79 . . . chaired Voters for Reagan-Bush in 1980 . . . Reagan's assistant for public liaison, 1981-83 . . . secretary of transportation, 1983-87 . . . married to Senate Minority Leader Robert Dole, R-Kan.

hope that Bush would be more willing to compromise on labor issues than Reagan had been. To that end, Dole was "an excellent choice," said Sen. Edward M. Kennedy, D-Mass., chairman of the Senate Labor and Human Resources Committee. AFL-CIO President Lane Kirkland said, "She is a person of proven stature and wide experience in public life who will give the Labor Department an important voice in the affairs of interest to working Americans." The U.S. Chamber of Commerce's vice president for domestic policy, Jeff H. Joseph, said, "We're pleased because she's a well-regarded pro who will do a good job managing the department."

Perhaps most important, however, was the unsurprising endorsement by Dole's husband, Sen. Robert Dole of Kansas, Bush's bitter rival for the Republican presidential nomination. As the Senate Republican leader, Dole was the person Bush needed most to help push his legislative program in Congress.

Bush said he did "not necessarily" recruit Elizabeth Dole to make peace with her husband. But, he added, "if there's a dividend in there, I'd accept it." Her selection also helped Bush meet his stated goal of tapping women for top posts. Dole was the only woman among Bush's cabinet members. However, another woman, Carla A. Hills, was named U.S. international trade representative, a job that is accorded cabinet rank—even though, strictly speaking, she is not in the cabinet.

A former Democrat, Elizabeth Dole had held jobs in the federal government over a span of twenty years and five administrations. Under Presidents Lyndon B. Johnson and Richard Nixon, she worked in consumer affairs. In 1973 Nixon placed her on the Federal Trade Commission, where she remained through the administrations of Gerald Ford and Jimmy Carter. She left that post in 1979 to help in her husband's 1980 presidential campaign.

Reagan hired her in 1981 as his public liaison to constituent groups. It was a job in which, Bush noted, she "had a lot of contact ... with the great labor leaders of this country." Two years later, Reagan made her secretary of transportation. After initial good reviews there, she departed amid a flurry of negative publicity in late 1987, when she once again left office to join her husband's presidential campaign. Critics said her tenure was marked more by style than by substance.

A magazine cover story the month she quit was bannered: "Charming her way to the White House: air travel stinks, auto safety's a joke and Washington still loves Liddy Dole." The chairman of the House Aviation Subcommittee, Rep. Norman Y. Mineta, D-Calif., said in 1985 that he was "frustrated by her lack of leadership." A committee Republican, Rep. Bud Shuster of Pennsylvania, said her efforts for airline safety were "too little, too late." Bush, however, hailed Dole's record and experience, saying she was the best person to handle the challenges of a "work force in dramatic change, with women, especially, continuing to enter ... in ever larger numbers."

Jack F. Kemp
Secretary of HUD

Jack French Kemp, a pro football quarterback mostly with the Buffalo Bills, retired from that game in 1970 and moved immediately into politics. That year he was elected to Congress from a suburban Buffalo district, which he represented through 1988. In 1989 he devoted his energies to his unsuccessful quest for the Republican presidential nomination.

Judged by legislative action, Kemp's first decade in Congress was not notable. He never had the patience to haggle over amendments or sit through long debates on the floor. Often he was not even there. But

Jack F. Kemp

Paul Conklin

Born in Los Angeles July 13, 1935 ... graduated from Occidental College, 1957 ... Army Reserve, 1958-62 ... professional football quarterback, 1957-70, with San Diego Chargers and Buffalo Bills; won two American Football League championships and one AFL most valuable player award ... cofounded AFL Players Association and was its president, 1965-70 ... elected to U.S. House of Representatives in 1970 to represent Buffalo, New York, suburbs, reelected through 1986 ... elected Republican Conference chairman, 1981 ... entered Republican presidential primary, 1987; withdrew March 10, 1988 ... married, with four children.

Kemp had the idea of "supply-side economics" —to make broad and deep tax cuts as a way of stimulating the economy and increasing federal revenues. He also persuaded 1980 presidential candidate Ronald Reagan to accept the idea.

The first year of Reagan's presidency, in 1981, was a triumph for Kemp. Although he was without a senior position on any committee that handled the budget or Reagan's tax-cut measure that year, he was the most important congressional force in their passage. Kemp had achieved the unusual feat of becoming a leader in the House by becoming a leader on the outside first. In recognition of his accomplishment, he was elected as chairman of the House Republican conference.

Kemp was well-positioned to cater to the GOP's conservative wing, and he often did so. His views on defense and foreign policy placed him firmly in the conservative tradition. In the realm of social policy, the congressman also bore some distinctive conservative earmarks. However, he seldom made the litmus-test social issues his first priority. In 1984 Kemp made headlines in Buffalo by refusing to cross a picket line. He helped earn the president's support for federally aided "enterprise zones" in impoverished urban areas. And he sponsored legislation to permit public-housing tenants to join together to buy their dwellings from the government.

At Kemp's swearing-in ceremony as HUD secretary on February 13, 1989, President Bush mentioned both enterprise zones and tenant ownership among "our goals" of bringing jobs and investment to the inner cities, and "finally end[ing] the tragedy of homelessness. . . . Jack's a man of ideas, and I've made clear that I want him to apply his creativity and energy to the area of housing and urban policy."

Manuel Lujan, Jr.
Secretary of the Interior

In 1985, after being passed over by President Reagan for the job of secretary of

Manuel Lujan, Jr.

Born in San Ildefonso, New Mexico, May 12, 1928, to prominent Hispanic family . . . father was mayor of Santa Fe . . . graduated from College of Santa Fe . . . worked briefly as broker for family's insurance agency . . . ran unsuccessfully for state Senate in 1964 . . . first and only Hispanic Republican member of U.S. House of Representatives, 1969-89 . . . ranking Republican on Interior and Insular Affairs Committee, 1981-85, then on Science, Space, and Technology Committee, 1985-89 . . . married, with four children.

the interior, Rep. Manuel Lujan, Jr., seemed to abandon all hope of getting the post. He gave up his ranking position on the House Interior and Insular Affairs Committee and did not seek reelection in 1988. He had planned to sell his Washington condominium and return home to Albuquerque.

Instead, Bush unexpectedly offered Lujan the job he had long wanted. In Lujan, Bush chose a man who not only added Hispanic representation in the cabinet—in addition to Secretary of Education Lauro F. Cavazos—but whose inclinations matched the president's. Both were non-confrontational pragmatists, generally on the side of private enterprise in questions of public land use, but willing to listen to, if not support, conservationists' concerns.

Lujan spent his twenty years in Congress struggling with the requirements of party loyalty and pressure from environmentalists at home. More often than not, he quietly voted with his party on environmental issues, yet still disappointed many Republicans who wanted a greater show of partisanship. He was more likely to side with environmentalists when the issue involved New Mexico. "Lujan has always been far more moderate on local environmental issues than on western or national issues," said Debbie Sease, a lobbyist for the Sierra Club. Overall, he voted with the environmentalists only 18 percent of the time between 1973 and 1988, according to the League of Conservation Voters.

In 1981 the Interior Department infuriated Lujan by quietly leasing seven hundred acres of New Mexico wilderness for oil and gas development. Lujan drafted a proposal to prohibit any such future leases, but he backed off when Interior Secretary James G. Watt assured him it would not happen again. On matters farther from home, Lujan backed the Reagan administration by voting to reduce federal subsidies for water projects, to limit the liability of utilities in nuclear accidents, and to remove most restrictions on mineral leasing of wilderness lands after the year 2000.

As far back as 1970, Lujan was arguing that federal lands should be opened up to more grazing, timber cutting, and mining, as well as recreation. "I don't see why

we can't all exist together," he said at the time. He also had been a strong defender of western water projects. Although Lujan voted for environmentally oriented Alaska land legislation in 1979, he cosponsored a bill that would have permitted development in Alaska's Arctic National Wildlife Refuge. He fought to soften federal controls on strip mining, and he opposed a 1977 strip-mining control bill, which passed the House on a vote of 241-64. On the other hand, he voted with an overwhelming House majority to override Reagan's veto of the Clean Water bill.

Business groups praised the choice of Lujan. Charles J. DiBona, president of the American Petroleum Institute, said that Lujan should make "an excellent secretary of the interior." Conservationists generally expressed disappointment. "We expected more of Mr. Bush," said Ken Maize of Friends of the Earth. "Mr. Lujan has a very bad environmental record going back many years." Sease struck a more conciliatory note: "He has a pretty poor environmental record, but we have worked with him on occasion. We've always had access to him." She suggested that, as secretary with a "different mandate" than that of a member of Congress, he might prove more pro-environment.

Lujan's non-ideological style and background in Congress suggested he would have a smoother tenure at Interior than Watt, the militantly prodevelopment secretary who beat him out for the job in 1981 and served until 1983.

In a confirmation hearing before the Senate Energy Committee on January 26, 1989, Lujan said that he would support Bush's decisions once they were made but would argue Interior's case vigorously while policy was being made. "I don't intend to be a shrinking violet," he said.

"I will not permit mining, drilling, or timber harvesting in the national parks and wilderness areas," he said. Under question-

Robert A. Mosbacher

Susan Muniak

Born in White Plains, New York, March 11, 1927 ... attended the Choate School in Wallingford, Connecticut, and Washington and Lee University in Lexington, Virginia ... moved to Houston to manage father's oil investments ... independent oil and gas producer with fortune estimated at over $200 million ... chief fund raiser for President Ford's 1976 campaign and Bush's 1980 and 1988 presidential campaigns ... international yachting champion ... married to Georgette Paulsin, a former model who is principal owner and chief executive of La Prairie, a cosmetics company ... has four children by first wife, who died in 1970.

law—where "valid existing rights" predated the creation of a park. Lujan's immediate predecessor, Donald P. Hodel, proposed rules allowing additional claims. Lujan said he would seek to trade such rights for other federal mineral rights.

Robert A. Mosbacher
Secretary of Commerce

The post at Commerce traditionally had been seen as a backwater, a low-visibility job. However, the secretary's main task—promoting American business growth—had assumed greater significance in recent years because of America's foreign-trade deficit.

"That is the overwhelming challenge facing him," said Lloyd Bentsen, D-Texas, chairman of the Senate Finance Committee. "That's No. 1, 2, and 3." Friends and associates said that, as one who had amassed a fortune in the high-risk and hotly competitive oil-wildcatter business, Mosbacher was unlikely to be sympathetic to any efforts by the Democratic-controlled Congress to restrict foreigners' access to U.S. markets. Still, they added, he was willing to extend government help to private enterprise.

At his confirmation hearing before the Senate Commerce Committee, Mosbacher came under fire for his role as chief fund raiser in Bush's 1988 presidential campaign (as he had been in Bush's 1980 campaign and Gerald Ford's in 1976). Mosbacher was asked about failing to provide full disclosure concerning efforts to solicit so-called "soft-money" contributions outside of the federal campaign-finance reporting system. But Sen. Ernest F. Hollings, D-S.C., the committee's chairman, said Mosbacher did nothing illegal or improper, and he blamed Congress for not enacting stricter campaign-finance laws. The Senate voted unanimously (100-0) on January 31 to confirm the appointment. Upon taking office,

ing by committee members, the declaration was less definitive than it sounded. Mining in parks was already banned by law. A controversy arose over an exception to that

Mosbacher promptly challenged the State and Defense departments in an effort to make commercial considerations more important in foreign policy and national security decisions. He opposed a Pentagon-supported plan to let Japan build a fighter plane modeled on the American F-16. He sought to persuade the president that without safeguards in the deal, Japan could apply fighter technology to the development of a strong civilian aircraft industry that someday could rival America's.

On another matter, Mosbacher appealed to Congress to make the Commerce Department a full partner with the State Department in deciding what technology could and could not be exported. American businesses had complained that the State Department was slow to act on export requests, and that there was no appeal from an unfavorable ruling.

Samuel K. Skinner
Secretary of Transportation

Samuel K. Skinner had a background in mass transportation, a record as a tough prosecuting attorney, and a pilot's all-weather license. But it was probably his political connections that won him his job as secretary of transportation.

Skinner's political mentor was Gov. James R. Thompson of Illinois, who helped deliver the state to Bush in both the 1988 Republican primary and the general election. Their association began in 1971 when Skinner worked for then U.S. attorney Thompson. Together they successfully prosecuted former Democratic governor Otto Kerner for corruption. As governor, Thompson named Skinner as chair of the Regional Transportation Authority of Northeastern Illinois, the nation's second-largest commuter mass-transportation system.

As the man in charge of the Department of Transportation, Skinner would need all the political prowess he could muster.

Samuel K. Skinner

Born in Chicago June 10, 1938 . . . received accounting degree from University of Illinois in 1960 . . . Army officer, 1960-61 . . . worked in marketing and management at IBM Corp., 1961-68, while earning law degree at DePaul University . . . assistant U.S. attorney for Northern District of Illinois, 1968-75, and U.S. attorney, 1975-77 . . . senior partner in Chicago law firm of Sidley & Austin . . . served 1984-89 as chairman of Regional Transportation Authority of Northeastern Illinois . . . Illinois co-chairman of Bush's 1980 presidential bid and 1988 Bush campaign . . . licensed pilot . . . married, with three children.

His main goal was to develop a national policy to account for transportation needs into the next century, he told separate congressional panels during confirmation hearings. He said such a policy would identify funding requirements for roads, bridges, and other elements of the transportation system.

Skinner also would face a renewed bid by some in Congress, led by Wendell H. Ford, D-Ky., chairman of Senate Commerce's Subcommittee on Aviation, to remove the Federal Aviation Administration from the department and establish it as an independent agency. Ford and many in the aviation industry believed the department often had subjected aviation policies and regulations to political manipulation. At the hearings, Skinner parried questions about the FAA's future status. Another aviation issue on the agenda was the effort to modernize the air-traffic-control system, a campaign that had been plagued by cost overruns, delays, and concerns about safety. At a press conference announcing his nomination, Skinner said, "Safety must always be our No. 1 priority."

Skinner's familiarity with transportation issues—not a characteristic of all secretaries of transportation—was welcomed by transportation lobbyists. The concerns of highway-industry groups that Skinner's experience as chairman of the Regional Transportation Authority of Northeastern Illinois might give him a mass-transit bias were tempered by his reputation as a pragmatist. Federal highway and transit programs are funded chiefly by a nine-cents-per-gallon gasoline tax, of which one penny goes to transit. Mass-transit people would like to increase their share. The highway lobby is concerned about funding the Interstate Highway System after legislation expires in fiscal 1991.

Skinner was credited with working well with Democrats and Republicans on the Illinois transit board and with putting the financially shaky Chicago transit program on sound ground. Peter Peyser, Jr., whose

Washington-based lobbying firm, Peyser Associates, represented the Chicago-area transit authority, said that Skinner "fits the Bush mold pretty well."

The only challenge to Skinner in the confirmation process came from Sen. Howard M. Metzenbaum, D-Ohio, who said that Skinner should explain why, as a prosecutor, he "failed to pursue allegations of fraudulent testing of NutraSweet," the artificial sweetener made by G.D. Searle & Co., and then later joined the firm that defended Searle in the case. Skinner said he "conducted himself in accordance with Department of Justice guidelines."

Louis W. Sullivan
Secretary of HHS

To head the vast Department of Health and Human Services (HHS), whose annual spending accounts for about one-third of the $1.3 trillion federal budget, Bush picked Dr. Louis W. Sullivan, president and founder of Morehouse School of Medicine in Atlanta. He became the only black member of the Bush cabinet.

Sullivan encountered a brief flap over his views on abortion and whether he could accept pay from the medical school for accumulated sabbatical leave that he had not taken. The abortion question arose when word leaked in mid-January that, during a courtesy call on Sen. Bob Packwood, R-Ore., Sullivan indicated he personally opposed overturning the Supreme Court's 1973 ruling, *Roe v. Wade,* that legalized abortion. That position seemed to put Sullivan at odds with Bush who, a few days earlier, assured abortion foes that the nominee supported their call for a constitutional amendment to outlaw abortion.

Packwood, who was prochoice, was the ranking Republican on the Senate Finance Committee, which had scheduled hearings on Sullivan's nomination. Bush restated his support of Sullivan, and administration offi-

Louis W. Sullivan

R. Michael Jenkins

Born in Atlanta, Georgia, November 3, 1933 ... graduated with high honors from Morehouse College in Atlanta in 1954 ... received M.D. from Boston University in 1958 ... codirector of hematology, Boston University Medical Center, 1966-75 ... professor, later dean, director, and, 1985-89, president of the Morehouse School of Medicine ... member of myriad educational, medical, and scientific organizations, including the National Cancer Institute's National Cancer Advisory Board ... prominent medical researcher, specializing in blood disorders related to vitamin deficiencies ... married, with three children.

Senate's anti-abortion activists, said after the meeting that he was prepared to support Sullivan's nomination. Humphrey attributed the discrepancies in Sullivan's statements to the fact that "someone with no public experience tends to get into trouble until he learns the ways of this jungle." But another right-to-life advocate at the meeting, Sen. Jesse Helms, R-N.C., was less sanguine. "Some of my confusion has been relieved, but not all of it," said Helms, adding that he still was eager to hear what Sullivan would have to say in his confirmation hearings.

Appearing before the Senate Finance Committee on February 23, he assured the senators that his views on abortion were identical to Bush's: that he opposed abortion and federal funding for it except in cases of rape, incest, or danger to the mother's life. Moreover, he said he favored a reversal of *Roe v. Wade*. Still unsatisfied, Helms cast the only nay vote on March 1 when the Senate approved Sullivan's nomination 98-1.

On the matter of sabbatical-leave pay from Morehouse, the White House announced on February 4 that Sullivan had agreed to forgo any payment from the school in order, he said, "to preclude even the remotest possibility of any appearance that my actions as Secretary might be influenced due to outside income." Several members of the Senate Finance Committee said his forfeiture of this pay was unduly harsh because it had been earned before his government service began. On March 29 the Office of Government Ethics said it had approved an agreement permitting him to receive $215,000 of the $300,000 amount that he was owed for sabbaticals.

Dick Thornburgh
Attorney General

Bush's decision to keep Dick Thornburgh as attorney general contrasted

cials hastily arranged for Sullivan to meet with the Senate's Republican leadership and prominent anti-abortion lawmakers. Gordon J. Humphrey, R-N.H., one of the with the practices of some recent presidents, notably Reagan, Nixon, and John F. Kennedy, who named close friends, relatives, or top political associates as the nation's chief law officer. While Thornburgh and Bush had worked together, the attorney general was not among Bush's close advisers.

Thornburgh came to the job from the Institute of Politics, which he had directed at Harvard University's Kennedy School of Government after he left the governorship of Pennsylvania. As a Republican two-term governor (1978-86), his views were marked more by pragmatism than ideology. Before that, as U.S. attorney in his hometown of Pittsburgh and then as head of the Justice Department's Criminal Division in the Ford administration, he won a reputation for rooting out corruption and white-collar crime. Thornburgh came into the Justice Department's top job in August 1988, succeeding Reagan's close friend and adviser Edwin Meese III, who resigned amid criticism over his conduct of the office. At Thornburgh's swearing-in August 12, Reagan emphasized that his new attorney general would be heavily involved in a "war on drugs." And "you're just the man I want" to lead the anti-drug effort, the president said. Thornburgh, in turn, pledged to sustain "a vigorous effort to make drug trafficking and drug abuse public enemy number one."

Expressing his endorsement of that goal, Thornburgh became the first attorney general in eight years to argue a case before the Supreme Court, urging the justices to uphold a drug-testing program. However, early in the Bush administration, the attorney general locked horns with William J. Bennett, the new "drug czar," over a jurisdictional matter—a "turf battle" in the parlance of bureaucratic infighting.

Thornburgh drew political fire from Congress by persuading Reagan to pocket veto a bill to bolster the legal protection for "whistleblowers" —government employees who inform on what they perceive to be waste, fraud, or abuse in their agencies. The attorney general contended that the bill was

Dick Thornburgh

Born in Pittsburgh July 16, 1932 ... graduated from Yale in 1954, and from University of Pittsburgh law school with high honors in 1957 ... was in private law practice in Pittsburgh, 1959-69, with Kirkpatrick & Lockhart ... U.S. attorney for the Western District of Pennsylvania, 1969-75 ... headed Criminal Division of Justice Department, 1975-77 ... elected governor of Pennsylvania in 1978; reelected in 1982 ... in 1987 became director of the Institute of Politics at Harvard University's John F. Kennedy School of Government, and returned to Kirkpatrick & Lockhart ... married, with four sons.

unconstitutional because it set up situations in which the government would sue itself. In 1989, after intense negotiations between Thornburgh and congressional sponsors of new whistleblower legislation the House passed a compromise bill with his blessing.

He endeared himself to anti-abortion groups by approving a Supreme Court brief that argued for overturning the 1973 *Roe v. Wade* decision, which made abortion legal nationwide. Although he was a holdover from the previous administration, Thornburgh expected to bring new people into the department. It would "be a mistake not to have substantial turnover," he said.

The department that Thornburgh inherited from Meese was considered the most politicized of all the cabinet-level agencies. Thornburgh insisted that in making appointments at Justice, and in recommending federal judgeship nominations to the president, there would be no ideological "litmus test." On the other hand, he said he would look for judges who "interpret the law rather than make it" —which could be interpreted as code language for a conservative judicial agenda.

Recalling that Thornburgh's appointment initially brought dismay to the Republican right, the British magazine *Economist* commented in February that the attorney general, in taking several conservative positions, "is proving to be the surprise of the Bush cabinet."

James D. Watkins
Secretary of Energy

Bush sought to get a grip on the nation's problem-plagued weapons-reactor complex by appointing a former nuclear submarine skipper and well-regarded trouble-shooter, James D. Watkins, as secretary of energy. Admiral Watkins, who retired from the Navy in 1986 as chief of naval operations, won high marks in 1988 in his first civilian job—taking over a dissension-

James D. Watkins

R. Michael Jenkins

Born in Alhambra, California, March 7, 1927 ... graduated from U.S. Naval Academy, 1949; Naval Submarine School, 1951; and Naval Postgraduate School, 1958 ... administrative assistant, Atomic Energy Commission, 1962-64 ... executive officer of USS *Long Beach*, Navy's first nuclear-powered surface ship, 1967-69 ... chief of naval personnel, 1975-78 ... commander, Sixth Fleet, 1978-79 ... commander in chief, U.S. Pacific Fleet, 1981-82 ... chief of naval operations, 1982-86 ... retired with rank of admiral, 1986 ... chairman, Presidential Commission on the HIV Epidemic, 1987-88 ... married, with six children.

torn presidential commission on AIDS and hammering out a firm set of recommendations.

His job at the Department of Energy

was likely to be even tougher. He had to try to maintain the strength of the U.S. nuclear arsenal while undertaking an overhaul and cleanup—projected to cost between $100 billion and $200 billion—of the aging reactors that supplied it. Bush said he expected Watkins to address the problems with little or no increase in spending.

Watkins's Navy service gave him a useful background in nuclear energy—a key criterion for Bush. After attending Naval Submarine School, he shipped out on the first of many submarine tours, including a stint as commanding officer of the nuclear attack submarine *Snook*. He studied further at the Oak Ridge (Tennessee) School of Reactor Technology in 1958 and at the Atomic Energy Commission's Division of Naval Reactors in 1966-67. During the 1960s he spent several years on the staff of Admiral Hyman G. Rickover, father of the nuclear navy.

After retirement from the Navy, Watkins won acclaim for his political and administrative leadership of the embattled presidential commission on AIDS. The panel was in shambles—its credibility under fire, its commissioners bickering over direction—when Watkins became its second chairman in 1987. He was credited with turning the foundering commission into a noteworthy success, through a mixture of strong leadership, consensus-building, long hours on the job, good staff work, and personal intelligence.

The panel's final recommendations, which were issued in June 1988, included a call for federal legislation prohibiting discrimination against those carrying the virus that causes AIDS. Bush broke with the Reagan administration and endorsed the entire package of recommendations almost immediately.

Partly because of the admiral's admitted inexperience with fossil fuels, his nomination was cautiously received by oil and gas industry executives, and some members

of Congress. Bush said he would encourage the appointment of petroleum experts for second-level posts at the Department of Energy, but would leave that decision to Watkins.

Both the Senate Energy Committee and the full Senate unanimously confirmed Watkins. Sen. J. Bennett Johnston, D-La., the committee chairman, told his fellow senators that the job entrusted to Watkins was "perhaps the most daunting challenge that we have ever given anybody in the cabinet."

Clayton Yeutter
Secretary of Agriculture

Clayton Yeutter came to the top job at the Department of Agriculture armed with a law degree, a doctorate in agricultural economics, and first-hand experience both in Washington bureaucracy and on his family's Nebraska farm. For the last two and a half years of the Reagan administration, he was its hard-hitting point man in international trade relations. Yeutter, a blunt-spoken, robust six-footer with a booming voice and friendly, physical manner, noted with obvious pride that his name rhymes with "fighter."

In 1985 Yeutter had become the U.S. trade representative with the dual duties of fighting for an expansion of U.S. markets abroad and against attempts in a protectionist-minded Congress to dilute America's free-trade policies. As the newly designated secretary of agriculture, he preached a message that appealed to senators—and quickly won their approval of his appointment. At his confirmation hearings he said that boosting U.S. agriculture required a determined effort to expand America's share of food exports in world markets. Trade expansion clearly remained at the top of his agenda.

While there was general agreement on that view, further testimony caused some members of Congress to ask whether he or

Clayton K. Yeutter

Paul Conklin

Born in Eustis, Nebraska, December 10, 1930 ... graduated from the University of Nebraska and served five years in the Air Force ... returned to Nebraska as a rancher ... returned to the university for a law degree in 1963 and a doctorate in agricultural economics in 1966 ... executive assistant to Gov. Norbert Tiemann in 1966-68 ... at the Department of Agriculture, administered the Consumer and Marketing Service, 1970-71; quit to become regional director of President Nixon reelection campaign in 1972; returned as assistant secretary in 1973-75 ... deputy U.S. trade representative in 1975-77 ... president of the Chicago Mercantile Exchange in 1978-85; U.S. trade representative in 1985-86.

Richard G. Darman, director of the Office of Management and Budget, was directing farm policy. On February 28, Darman told the Senate Appropriations Committee he favored overhauling farm commodity programs in 1989 to achieve budgetary savings rather than wait for the farm law to expire in 1990. But Yeutter, in appearances before two House committees the same week, saw the matter in a different light. He said that international trade negotiations in which the administration was seeking the removal of all "trade-distorting" agricultural subsidies would not be completed before the end of 1990. Therefore, he said, any major change in U.S. farm programs should be delayed until then. Noting the discrepancy, Senate Agriculture Committee Chairman Patrick J. Leahy, D-Vt., asked Darman in writing whether he was "speaking for the administration in terms of the timing of new commodity programs."

Administration sources said Yeutter was still formulating his strategy for achieving agriculture budget cuts. He would say only that he would propose ways to achieve the president's goal of reducing federal spending on agriculture by $1.1 billion in fiscal year 1990.

A deeper concern among farm-state members of Congress was whether Yeutter's free-market leanings would dissuade him from using policy levers to assist farmers. At Yeutter's confirmation hearing before the Senate Agriculture Committee, he referred to farm-income supports being a "safety net" for farmers. His home-state senator, Robert Kerrey, D-Neb., objected that "the program was set up to keep the price up," not merely to fill cracks that the market creates.

Yeutter also said that, despite reports of trading fraud at the Chicago Mercantile Exchange and the Chicago Board of Trade, "no significant changes" were required in the regulatory structure of the futures markets. There had been legislation to shift some regulation to the Securities and Exchange Commission from the Commodity Futures Trading Commission. Yeutter, president of the Chicago Mercantile Exchange from 1978 to 1985, said he had been unaware of any fraud, although a federal investigation reportedly began during his last year there.

Before going to Chicago, Yeutter served two stints in the Agriculture Department, first as director of the Consumer and Marketing Service and then as assistant to Secretary Earl L. Butz in the Nixon presidency. During 1972, between the two jobs, Yeutter directed the president's reelection campaign in the Midwest.

Yeutter grew up on a 2,500-acre "corn and cow" farm on land that his grandfather settled in wind-swept central Nebraska. But Yeutter had had little time to spend on the family farm during his adult life. He took his undergraduate, law, and doctoral degrees at the University of Nebraska, served in the Air Force five years, and practiced law in Lincoln, the state capital.

13

Executive Office of the President

To head his White House staff, President Bush chose John H. Sununu, a man who lacked Washington experience but impressed Bush with his take-charge personality. As the governor of New Hampshire—he completed his third term in 1988—Sununu greatly aided Bush in a crucial period during his quest for the presidency.

Having lost to Sen. Robert Dole of Kansas in the 1988 nominating season's first event, the Iowa caucus, Bush entered New Hampshire's "first in the nation" presidential primary in great need of a victory to sustain his campaign. He did achieve a victory, with the governor's considerable help.

Going on to take the Republican party's nomination at New Orleans in August, Bush again received assistance from Sununu in the fall campaign against Democratic foe Michael S. Dukakis, who, as governor of Massachusetts, had incurred Sununu's wrath over several regional issues. Sununu brought to the White House job strong conservative credentials, pleasing to members of the Republican right who remained uneasy about Bush's middle-of-the-road tendencies.

For the key post of budget director—formally director of the Office of Management and Budget (OMB)—Bush looked to a veteran Washington insider, Richard G.

Darman, a political moderate who had close associations with James A. Baker III, the new secretary of state who had managed Bush's 1988 campaign.

Another insider, Brent Scowcroft, returned to a job he had held under President Gerald R. Ford, that of chairman of the national security council. As the president's national security adviser, Scowcroft held a position that some former occupants—particularly Henry A. Kissinger and Zbigniew Brzezinski—had made a base of power, challenging the secretary of state's authority.

That mode of operation had not been Scowcroft's, however. Furthermore, he served with Baker and Secretary of Defense Dick Cheney in the Ford administration, and all three were reputed to be close friends. Still another Ford connection surfaced among Bush's key executive appointments. Carla A. Hills, whom he named U.S. trade representative, was an assistant attorney general and then secretary of housing and urban development in the Ford administration. Reagan holdovers include CIA Director William H. Webster and White House Press Secretary Marlin Fitzwater.

Profiles of key appointees in the Executive Office of the President, along with those of the president and vice president, follow:

George Bush
President

George Bush laid claim to extensive experience in public office. After an early adulthood making his fortune in the oil-development business, he went on to become a veritable handyman of U.S. politics. Beginning in 1967, he served four years in the U.S. House of Representatives from Texas. Although he failed in two races for the U.S. Senate from Texas, in 1964 and 1970, the result of the second loss was that Bush became a politician by appointment rather than election.

He followed his second Senate defeat over the next six years with stints as U.S. ambassador to the United Nations (1971-73), chairman of the Republican National Committee (1973-74), head of the U.S. liaison office (later embassy) in Peking (1974-75), and director of central intelligence (1976-77).

The appointments by Presidents Richard Nixon and Gerald R. Ford undoubtedly shaped his philosophy, yet Bush's appreciation of centrist politics was most evident in his brief career in the House. There he avoided extremes, shunned shrill pronouncements, and often put something in his speeches that appealed to almost everyone.

Beneath his rhetoric, his voting record basically was conservative. His affluent constituents from Houston's seventh congressional district would not have it any other way; as of 1989 it was still the most Republican district in Texas. Nevertheless, there was some evidence of more moderate leanings in Bush's voting record. The most notable was his vote for the Civil Rights Act of 1968 and the open-housing requirements in it. At the same time, Bush qualified his support, saying he would like to amend the bill and "remedy some of the inequities in the open-housing section." He soon distanced himself from any image of all-out civil rights advocacy.

Bush's ability to balance progressive and conservative agendas also was seen in his proposals for environmental protection and political reform. Bush typically called for "responsible" action in both areas. In fiscal outlook, he was orthodox Republican. As a member of the House Ways and Means Committee in 1967, he cosponsored the ultimately unsuccessful Human Investment Act, which was intended to alleviate poverty through tax incentives instead of federal grants. He opposed tax reform of the progressive variety. He consistently supported the oil industry, as any Texan in Congress felt compelled to do.

More Yankee than Cowboy

Though he became a Texas oil man after college, Bush's bouts of intermittent moderation revealed him to be more New England yankee than cowboy businessman. He still resembled the suave Ivy Leaguer, not the Sun Belt merchant. Born George Herbert Walker Bush in Milton, Massachusetts (June 12, 1924), the son of an investment banker, Prescott Bush, he would grow up amid wealth—though not great wealth—and a strong family sense of public service. His father, a Republican, served Connecticut in the U.S. Senate for ten years, 1952-62. Young George Bush followed many other privileged youths by attending one of New England's elite prep schools, in this case Phillips Academy in Andover, Massachusetts.

But he did not pursue the special dispensations of a silver spoon upbringing when World War II came. On his eighteenth birthday, Bush enlisted in the Navy and became a pilot, the youngest at that time. He flew combat missions in the Pacific and won the Navy's Distinguished Flying Cross for completing a bombing attack after his plane was hit by flak. Two crewmen died when the plane was ditched at sea.

He returned home a war hero, attended Yale University, captaining its baseball team and completing a degree in two and a half years. Upon graduation in 1948, he and his wife, Barbara, moved to Texas. He entered the oil business, and they raised a family of five children. Bush wanted to learn the business from the ground up, taking his first jobs as a warehouse sweeper, and then supply salesman, with an oil-field supply company in Odessa, Texas, of which his father was a director.

In 1951 he helped start a company that traded oil leases and royalties, and two years later cofounded Zapata Petroleum Corporation, first based in Midland, Texas, and then Houston. It was in Houston that Bush became active in Republican affairs and served as chairman of the GOP organization in Harris County. In 1964, in his first political race, Bush failed to unseat Ralph Yarborough, the state's liberal Democratic senator. But two years later, he won a House seat that had been newly created in the Houston suburbs.

George Bush

Formative Years in Congress

Bush was one of fifty-nine Republican freshmen elected in 1966, the biggest crop of Republicans in the House in two decades. Beyond its size, this class mattered because the party's ranks in the House had dwindled to a post-Depression low. In 1967 nearly every third Republican representative was a freshman. The newcomers were generally viewed as more progressive than their predecessors.

Unlike some of their forebears, and unlike many who would come to Congress in the Reagan Revolution, the class of 1966 was not hostile to the federal government. Those members saw the New Deal as a settled issue, and some even supported the Great Society programs of the Johnson administration.

Many were from cities or from relatively new suburban districts, and many were from the region later to be known as the Sun Belt. This represented an incipient shift away from the party's traditional base in the small towns and rural areas of the Northeast and the Midwest. Bush, a transplanted New Englander elected from Houston's western neighborhoods and suburbs, was part of this trend.

Thomas S. Kleppe, a North Dakota Republican, a classmate and close friend who later became President Ford's secretary of the interior, recalled Bush as a class standout from the start. "In the first place he was bright; he didn't have that Phi Beta Kappa key by accident," Kleppe said. And Bush had political acumen that belied his lack of experience in elective office.

Bush also was blessed with some extraordinary political assets. The first of these was that he had won a seat in Texas, a big and growing state where the Republican party had been all but shut out since Reconstruction. There had been no incumbent, as Bush's district had just been created in a court-ordered redistricting. It was composed largely of Houston precincts that he had carried in an unsuccessful attempt to win a Senate seat in 1964.

The state's House delegation at the time included no Republicans at all. So Bush's campaign attracted a visit by Ford, then the House Republican leader. And Richard Nixon, then a former vice president, came to help, as he had in Bush's 1964 race. When Bush won big, he became a symbol of his party's prospects in the new demographics of the Old South.

Another Republican, Robert D. Price, was elected from Texas that autumn. But it was Bush who had the strong story line— New England blueblood, decorated Navy flier in World War II, graduate of Yale and of the oil fields of west Texas. Bush promptly found himself a member of the Ways and Means Committee. Peter Roussel, a former Bush press secretary, said Bush was only the third freshman so favored in this century.

How did Bush become a Ways and Means member so fast? "I put him on," said Democrat Wilbur D. Mills of Arkansas, the committee's chairman of that era. "I got a phone call from his father telling me how much it mattered to him. I told him I was a Democrat and the Republicans had to decide; and he said the Republicans would do it if I just asked Jerry Ford." Mills recalled that he asked Ford and John W. Byrnes of Wisconsin, then the ranking Republican on the committee, and that was that.

Under Nixon's Tutelage

At the 1968 GOP convention that nominated Nixon for president, Bush was said to be on the four-name short list for vice president. He attributed that to the campaigning of his friends, but the seriousness of Nixon's consideration was widely attested. Certainly Nixon wanted to promote Bush in one way or another. Nixon urged the two-term House member (Bush was re-elected without opposition in 1968) to run for the Senate again in 1970.

After initial hesitation, he heeded Nixon's urging to run. The stakes in that race were high. Political commentator David Broder wrote in the *Washington Post* on October 27, 1970, that if Bush won he might well be Nixon's running mate in 1972 and the GOP presidential nominee in 1976. Instead, the Senate seat went to Lloyd Bentsen, who was to retain it into the Bush presidency, despite his own unsuccessful bid as the Democratic vice-presidential nominee in 1988. The loss to Bentsen, though, brought Bush a consolation prize, when Nixon named him U.S. representative to the United Nations.

"I was disappointed to see him go," Mills said. "Everybody seemed to like him. I guess he had it in his mind to be president even then." Mills also conferred his characteristic phrase of high praise: "He had the makings of a highly valuable member."

As for his record while a member of Congress, Bush stuck to a moderate path. Having made his fortune in oil in the 1950s and 1960s, he divested his holdings when he entered Congress. But his district's economy, and the state's, lived and died with the petroleum industry, and his voting record reflected that fact of political life. "On oil, he was a Texan," said Allen Schick of the Urban Institute, a student of the House's fiscal process. "But he was in no way an extremist. What kind of people do you put on the money committees? They were people who were pretty mainstream within their parties."

Bush was also capable of casting remarkably difficult votes, the most noted of which was his vote for open-housing language in amendments to the Civil Rights Act. The vote came just after the riots that followed the assassination of the Rev. Dr. Martin Luther King, Jr., in April 1968. Kleppe remembered receiving a call from Nixon just before the vote came up. "He said he was calling me and calling George to tell us to vote for that bill," Kleppe recalled. "He said you don't ever want your record to show a 'no' vote on that bill."

Through most of his career, Bush was thought of as a moderate. Such perceptions probably relied less on his actual voting record than on his image. The image was a blend of eastern background and Texas politics. It was bolstered by his good-government standards of ethics (he filed a full disclosure of his assets and debts voluntarily in each year he served in Congress). But the image also reflected Bush's personal lack of interest in zealotry. He seemed to approach politics as the conventional mating of ambition and public service.

Diffident Political Entry

Although he was the son of a senator, the future president was not weaned on politics. "I was a late starter in politics because we weren't much of a political family when I was growing up," Bush had written. "The subject of politics seldom came up at family gatherings." Like his father, Bush launched his political career only after he was established in business. It was not any particular cause that lured him, but the need for a new challenge.

In his book *Looking Forward,* Bush writes as if he were sought for the job, and not the seeker. He says that he was "asked" by Houston Republican leaders in 1962 to run for the Harris County GOP chairmanship; that he was "persuaded" by the Texas GOP chairman to challenge Democratic Sen. Yarborough in 1964; and that he was "asked" by Nixon in 1973 to take over the chairmanship of the Republican National Committee from Robert Dole.

It was just a month after his 1970 defeat when President Nixon named Bush to the United Nations post. That set in motion the second phase of his career—a career by appointment—which continued until he unsuccessfully sought the Republican presidential nomination in 1980, losing to Ronald Reagan and accepting second place on the ticket. Concluding two vice-presidential terms, eight years in the office,

Bush cranked up another presidential campaign. This time he emerged victorious, over a field of Republican candidates in the party primaries and over Democratic nominee Dukakis in the general election.

Dan Quayle
Vice President

Plucked from relative obscurity by George Bush, Dan Quayle became the youngest (age forty-one) vice president since Richard Nixon assumed that office in 1953. Only thirty-nine years old when Dwight D. Eisenhower tapped him for the ticket, Nixon went on to be a prominent figure in the Republican party for years to come, appearing on five national ballots and capturing the presidency twice. It was said that Quayle, too, might follow in those footsteps—if he could overcome unfavorable publicity that greeted his vice-presidential candidacy and followed him through the election campaign.

Bush, assured of the 1988 presidential nomination, surprised the Republican National Convention in New Orleans by announcing that the previously unheralded senator from Indiana was the man he wanted on the ticket. The delegates dutifully obliged despite a rising furor over questions about Quayle's background and suitability for the office. Above all else was the question of whether family connections had enabled him to avoid the Vietnam War draft in 1969. He had served instead in a hometown National Guard unit that was never called to active duty.

As the grandson of the late Eugene Pulliam, a conservative Indiana newspaper publisher, Quayle was born with ties to the state's political and media establishment. Pulliam, who founded Central Newspapers Inc., bought the *Indianapolis Star* three years before Quayle was born. Central later acquired the city's other daily, the *News,* three smaller Indiana newspapers, and the

Sue Klemens

Dan Quayle

two major dailies in Phoenix, Arizona.

Quayle had a stake in the family trust that operated the publishing chain, which made him a millionaire many times over. "Life has been very good to me," Quayle said in 1981, "I never had to worry about where I was going to go." His family separately owns and operates the small daily *Herald-Press* in his hometown of Huntington. Quayle was the paper's associate publisher and a political unknown when he entered and unexpectedly won a congressional seat in 1976. He served two terms in the House and was twice elected to the Senate.

Appeal to Conservatives

Political analysts saw in Bush's choice of Quayle an attempt, on the one hand, to appeal to the political right, and, on the other, to use Quayle's obscurity as a foil to enhance his own stature. Teamed with Quayle, Bush created an impression very different from the one when he was at Reagan's side. After years as a thoroughly overshadowed second in command, Bush came across as seasoned and authoritative, at least by comparison with Quayle. Conser-

vatives, meanwhile, rejoiced in Quayle's selection. "We now have someone we can market to our people in terms of issues," said conservative activist Paul Weyrich.

There was little doubt about his conservative credentials. Quayle was one of the Reagan administration's strongest supporters. He voted in favor of Reagan's position 85 percent of the time. His voting record won high marks from conservative and business groups, low ones from liberal groups and organized labor. Quayle echoed the Reagan administration's "defense through strength" line, supporting the strategic defense initiative (SDI), production of the MX missile, and spending hikes for the Pentagon.

On domestic issues, he voted for school prayer and Reagan's judicial nominees, including the controversial nomination of Robert H. Bork for Supreme Court justice. Coming from the agricultural Midwest, Quayle supported a 1985 overhaul of farm programs that included income support for farmers and numerous special projects. In 1986, however, he opposed a $1 billion plan for financially strapped farmers because it exceeded budget limits.

The legislative achievement that Quayle highlighted in the 1988 presidential election campaign was the Job Training Partnership Act. The jobs program, which he helped devise in 1982, succeeded the expiring and oft-criticized Comprehensive Employment and Training Act (CETA). It placed greater reliance on the private sector to provide job training, and it abolished the old CETA program of public-service employment.

Early in his Senate career, Quayle rode out a spell of bad publicity. Allegations arose that while he was still in the House, he and two other legislators had shared a house with Paula Parkinson, a lobbyist who later posed for *Playboy* magazine. The three legislators later voted against a bill Parkinson opposed. They contended that their votes were based on the merits of the issue, and the Justice Department dropped an investigation into whether the votes had been traded for sexual favors. Quayle's insistence that he never had a relationship with Parkinson never had been refuted.

That episode perhaps helped prepare him for the inquisitional attention that followed his vice-presidential nomination. From the outset, Bush and his team seemed committed to keeping Quayle on the ticket. Most political observers agreed that almost nothing would be as damaging to Bush as dumping Quayle under fire. But a trickle of tales about Quayle soon made him a campaign liability. The Cleveland *Plain Dealer* reported that he had inflated his résumé. The paper said that Quayle's supposed job as chief investigator of consumer complaints for the Indiana attorney general (1970-71) did not exist at the time. Quayle, the newspaper said, was actually an entry-level researcher.

Guard Duty Controversy

Quayle's defense on the Guard issue was that "no rules were broken" to secure his place and that no special favors were granted on his behalf. Evidence from the period was sketchy and conflicting. The *Washington Post* reported Indiana's Guard was at full strength at the time of Quayle's entry. But the Indiana Guard said certain outfits, such as the headquarters unit Quayle joined, had vacancies.

Whether or not the help was necessary, Wendell Phillippi, editor of a newspaper owned by Quayle's family, had indeed stepped in. Phillippi, a former official of the Indiana National Guard, had called a friend who was its director of planning in 1969 and was assured a space would be reserved for Quayle. At the time, upon Quayle's graduation from DePauw University, he had already been called for the draft and had passed his pre-induction physical exam. Joining the Guard enabled him to enter the

Indiana University law school, from which he took a degree in 1974.

The negative impact of the Guard question appeared to have been diluted by the din of approval Quayle received from sympathetic audiences, such as members of a Veterans of Foreign Wars' convention on August 22. The Quayle story also seemed to lose more of its sting as each new poll was published. The election results in November confirmed that if Quayle's selection was a setback for the Bush campaign, it was not crippling.

Quayle's vice-presidential role did not emerge clearly during his first months in office. His senior staff members appeared more ideological than Bush's, and when the vice president spoke out publicly, his tone was often harsher than Bush's. On the subject of Quayle's willingness to be outspoken, an unidentified "senior White House official" was quoted in the *Washington Post* as saying: "Quayle is much more comfortable doing it than Bush was as vice president or is now. He [Bush] likes others to do it for him."

Michael J. Boskin
Chief Economic Adviser

Michael J. Boskin, chairman of President Bush's Council of Economic Advisers, was a self-described "moderate conservative" economist who came to Washington from Stanford University, where he directed the Center for Economic Policy Research. During the 1988 election campaign, he was one of Bush's economic advisers.

Although only forty-three years old when named to the post, Boskin already was widely recognized for studies on taxation, saving, and the Social Security program, and on the effect of government policy on the economy.

Under his predecessor, Beryl W. Sprinkel, the council had come under criticism for its rosy view of the national econo-

Michael J. Boskin

Born in New York City, September 23, 1945 . . . graduated from the University of California, Berkeley, with highest honors in 1967 and pursued graduate studies there in economics, taking his master's degree in 1968 and doctorate in 1971 . . . taught at Stanford University, 1971-88 . . . Wolford Professor of Economics at Stanford and director of the university's Center for Economic Policy Research, 1988 . . . previously served as a consultant and adviser to the White House and various governmental agencies and wrote extensively on economic issues in government . . . took office as chairman of the president's Council of Economic Advisers, February 2, 1989, upon receiving Senate confirmation . . . married.

my's potential for continued growth. The council's forecasts were used by the White House and Congress to minimize federal deficit projections.

While Boskin had criticized some Reagan fiscal policies, he also exhibited unswerving fealty to Bush, defending the president-elect's no-tax pledge in the face of the widespread view that some form of tax increase would be necessary to reduce the deficit. On that score, Boskin was not likely to follow the practice of his intellectual mentor, Harvard economist Martin Feldstein, who was the council's chairman before Sprinkel. Feldstein often departed publicly from the standard White House line by making bleak forecasts.

When asked at his confirmation hearing if he was convinced that Bush would not have to raise taxes, Boskin replied: "I'm absolutely certain in my heart of hearts that the budget deficit can be brought under control without a tax increase and that the surest, safest way to get the budget deficit under control is to slow the growth of government spending."

Boskin was one of the architects of Bush's "flexible freeze" plan for reducing the deficit. It essentially offered a status-quo budget plan that relied on continued economic growth of at least 3 percent a year to produce new revenues, and a concomitant 2 percent reduction in interest rates to cut costs. By the spring of 1989, interest rates were continuing on an upward movement that began the previous year, and few "mainstream" economists detected signs of economic growth as robust as Boskin was counting on.

Richard G. Darman
OMB Director

For his budget director, George Bush turned to Richard G. Darman, a forty-five-year-old investment banker and veteran Washington insider. A protégé of James A. Baker III, Darman, like Baker, had built a reputation as a mainstream Republican moderate. He was a political pragmatist who was reputedly always willing to negotiate.

"I look at it as a positive signal," Rep. Leon E. Panetta, D-Calif., chairman of the House Budget Committee, said of Darman's appointment. "What you're looking for in [budget negotiations] is someone who can operate like Jim Baker. Dick Darman is as close to Jim Baker as you can get."

Darman had showcased this talent as a deputy to Baker, first in the White House and then at the Treasury Department. He was a prime mover of Reagan's 1981 tax-cut proposals. Then in 1985 and 1986 he shepherded Reagan's sweeping tax-overhaul proposals through Congress.

Darman is a legislative tactician. Indeed, his propensity for complex game plans—devising contingencies for everything that could go wrong—earned him a Washington sobriquet. Howard H. Baker, the former Senate Republican leader and White House chief of staff, coined the term "Darmanesque" for such elaborate stratagems.

As OMB director, Darman became the point man for the Bush administration on virtually all fiscal issues. He was responsible not only for carrying any White House plan for reducing the budget deficit to Capitol Hill, but also for getting it passed. Bush's marching orders to Darman had been simple; he was to uphold the president's campaign pledge of not raising taxes. Some Republican budget veterans once thought Darman would try to find a way around the no-tax restriction. But Darman let Congress know he had gotten Bush's message.

In testimony before the Senate Government Affairs Committee on January 19, 1989, Darman essentially ruled out any effort to raise taxes, even by another name. He said he would apply the "duck test" to proposed revenue-raisers. "If it looks like a duck, walks like duck, and quacks like a duck, then it is a duck," he quipped—

Richard G. Darman

Teresa Zabala

Born in North Carolina to a prosperous New England family on May 10, 1943 . . . graduated from Harvard College and Harvard Business School . . . later was on the faculty of the Harvard School of Government . . . served as an aide to Elliot Richardson during the Nixon administration . . . was assistant secretary of commerce for policy in the Ford administration . . . in 1981 became assistant to the president and deputy to the chief of staff under President Reagan . . . in 1985 was named deputy Treasury secretary . . . left government to become managing director of Shearson Lehman Brothers in April 1987 . . . married, with two sons.

drawing the analogy to taxes that might be disguised as user fees or as excises.

If anyone could find ambiguity in Bush's words, it was probably Darman. He showed as much pride in the way he phrased solutions to knotty problems as in the solutions themselves. In fact, he didn't distinguish between the two. "In the end, all the substance and tactics come to the drafting of words, whether you're talking about a law, a regulation, an order, or a speech," he was quoted as saying in a February 1986 issue of the *New York Times Magazine*. "The trick is to arrange a context in which several competing politicians can step forward together to simultaneously share what credit and blame there is for something that's going to at least be ambiguous," he said.

The president on February 9 sent Congress a set of proposed revisions to the fiscal 1990 budget that Reagan had submitted only a month earlier. The revisions became known as "Darman's document." The new budget chief prepared the document with little or no advice from the various affected departments and agencies, many of which had been left leaderless while new top officials were being appointed and confirmed.

More than that, he was the mastermind of a plan for giving the president an opportunity to deal directly with Congress, and perhaps individually with its key members, during the opening round of the annual budget process. This resulted from the sparsity of specifics in the document as to where spending would be cut to meet legally imposed deficit ceilings. It would be a matter for the president and Congress to negotiate—an idea that the Democratic leadership appeared to accept somewhat reluctantly. Darman had thus made his mark in Washington during the very first weeks of the Bush administration.

Marlin Fitzwater
Press Secretary

Marlin Fitzwater was credited with setting a new standard of cordiality and cooperation in the White House press office after he replaced Larry Speakes as President Reagan's chief spokesman in January

Marlin Fitzwater

Bill Fitzpatrick, The White House

Born in Salina, Kansas, November 24, 1942 ... graduated from Kansas State University 1965 with a degree in journalism ... joined federal government as writer-editor for Appalachian Regional Commission, 1965-67 ... U.S. Air Force, 1968-70 ... speech-writing and press relations jobs in Department of Transportation, Environmental Protection Agency, and Treasury Department, 1970-83 ... deputy press secretary to the president, 1983-85 ... press secretary to the vice president, 1985-87 ... presidential press spokesman 1987 to present ... divorced, father of two.

1987. For the previous two years, Fitzwater had been press secretary for George Bush when he was vice president. Within three weeks of being elected president, Bush announced that Fitzwater would stay on.

Affable and unassuming, Fitzwater was a balding, stocky man known for his fondness for cigars and broad-brimmed hats. The headwear reflected his western background. He grew up in Salina, Kansas, and at age twenty became the editor of a weekly newspaper in the nearby small town of Lindborg. Three years later he took a journalism degree at Kansas State University while working part-time as an advertising salesman for the local Manhattan *Mercury*.

Upon graduation in 1965, Fitzwater turned down a job offer from the *Wall Street Journal* and instead sought employment in Washington, D.C., to be near his schoolteaching fiance. He went to work as a public-relations assistant for the Appalachian Regional Commission, one of Lyndon B. Johnson's anti-poverty agencies. It was the first in a string of government jobs that led to the White House, interrupted only by two years' duty in the Air Force.

Out of uniform, Fitzwater became a speechwriter at the Department of Transportation, and then did similar work for the Environmental Protection Agency. A Republican, he received his first political post in 1981 after Ronald Reagan became president. Fitzwater moved to the Treasury Department as a deputy director of public information. Soon thereafter, he took a pay cut to move to the White House as assistant to Speakes, the man he would later replace.

Carla A. Hills
U.S. Trade Representative

At the February 6, 1989, swearing-in of his U.S. trade representative, Carla A. Hills, President Bush spoke of his dedication to a global free-trade policy. "Ladies and gentlemen, the goal of this administration's trade policy, simply put, is to open markets, not close them; to fight protectionism, not give in to it." Hills would be in the forefront of this thrust, he made clear, and he extolled her abilities to carry out that assignment.

"She's a skilled negotiator with a

Carla A. Hills

Susan Muniak

Born in Los Angeles January 3, 1934, to a wealthy family ... graduated from Stanford University, 1955, and Yale Law School, 1958 ... studied at Oxford ... assistant U.S. attorney (Civil Division) in Los Angeles ... partner in law firm cofounded with husband in Los Angeles, 1962-74 ... author of a book on antitrust law ... an assistant U.S. attorney general, 1974-75 ... secretary of housing and urban development, 1975-77 ... codirector of Washington office of Weil Gotshal & Manges, prominent New York-based law firm ... married, with four children.

strong international background and extensive experience in government," the president said. "As I said when I nominated her, I can think of no one better suited to be America's minister of trade at home and abroad." The Senate Finance Committee unanimously concurred in her nomination (19-0 vote) on January 27, as did the full

Senate (100-0) four days later.

Hills, a Washington attorney, was no newcomer to government. She was secretary of housing and urban development in the Ford administration. Finance Committee members dismissed assertions by conservative businessman Anthony Harrigan that she should not be confirmed because her law firm, which lobbied for some foreign clients, had registered her as a foreign agent. They expressed satisfaction with

steps she and her husband, banker and financial consultant Roderick Hills, had taken to counter conflict-of-interest charges.

The committee's hearing focused almost exclusively on trade matters. Hills pledged to consult routinely with Congress and conduct tough negotiations with America's trading partners. She vowed to open foreign markets "with a crowbar or a handshake." Retaliation authorized by the 1988 omnibus trade bill (PL 100-418) would be used, not as an end in itself but to lend credibility to U.S. demands, Hills said.

Finance Chairman Lloyd Bentsen, D-Texas, who had questioned her lack of experience in trade, praised her for answering the committee's questions "with more specifics than I have normally heard from a person being confirmed."

Thomas R. Pickering
U.N. Representative

The selection of Thomas R. Pickering as the U.S. representative to the United Nations was one of the few genuine surprises of President Bush's appointments. There had been speculation that Bush, like most of the presidents before him, would install a political appointee in that post. Conservatives, in particular, had lobbied for Alan L. Keyes, a protégé of former U.N. representative Jeane J. Kirkpatrick. In the fall election campaign, Keyes ran a losing race against Paul S. Sarbanes for the Maryland Democrat's Senate seat.

Pickering was a career Foreign Service officer who held two particularly sensitive ambassadorial posts, in El Salvador and Israel, during the Reagan administration. He generally had won plaudits, even from critics of Reagan's policies. While he was in El Salvador, Pickering played a small role in a secret White House supply network for the Nicaraguan contra rebels. In July 1987 he told the special congressional committee investigating the Iran-contra affair that he

---

Thomas R. Pickering

Born in Orange, New Jersey, November 5, 1931 ... Bowdoin College, A.B. 1953, and Fletcher School of Law and Diplomacy, Tufts University, M.A. 1954 ... joined Foreign Service in 1959, serving in Tanzania and various Washington posts until 1974 ... ambassador to Jordan in 1974-78, Nigeria 1981-83, El Salvador 1983-85, and Israel 1985-88 ... carries ambassadorial rank as U.S. representative to the United Nations ... married, with two children.

had helped arrange one shipment of military supplies to the contras in late 1984 or early 1985.

Other State Department and CIA officials came under sharp criticism from Congress for their more extensive roles in the secret contra network, which violated legal prohibitions then in effect. However, congressional committees never singled out Pickering for blame.

Pickering also was ambassador to Jordan in the mid-1970s, assistant secretary of state for oceans and international environmental and scientific affairs in the Carter administration, and ambassador to Nigeria in 1981-83.

Brent Scowcroft
National Security Adviser

Brent Scowcroft, the new national security adviser, was among Bush's first appointments. In selecting Scowcroft, Bush turned to a veteran of Washington's defense and foreign policy establishment who had a track record of courting bipartisan congressional support for presidential policies. Scowcroft, a retired Air Force lieutenant general, held the same position during the Ford administration and came to be regarded as the model for security advisers who seek to give presidents advice without filtering it through their own ideological perspectives.

Scowcroft had a well-developed sense of how a president could craft decisions that would win broad political support, especially in Congress. Unlike his friend, Secretary of State Baker, Scowcroft had wide experience in, and had a detailed knowledge of, defense and foreign policy issues.

Bush praised Scowcroft's experience, citing in particular his ability to approach national security issues "on a bipartisan basis." Sen. Richard G. Lugar, R-Ind., a senior member of the Foreign Relations Committee, called Scowcroft "an extremely

Brent Scowcroft

Paul Hosefros/NYT Pictures

Born in Ogden, Utah, March 19, 1925 ... entered U.S. Army in 1943, was graduated from U.S. Military Academy in 1947 ... held numerous operational, administrative, and teaching positions in the military in the 1950s and 1960s ... received master's degree in 1953 and doctorate in 1967 in international relations from Columbia University ... entered White House in February 1972 as military assistant to the president, became deputy national security adviser in 1973, and was national security adviser from November 1975 until January 1977 ... retired from the Air Force in 1975 as a lieutenant general ... chaired President's Commission on Strategic Forces in 1983, member in 1985 of the President's Blue Ribbon Commission on Defense Management, and in 1986-87 of the Tower commission investigating the Iran-contra affair ... became vice chairman of Kissinger Associates Inc., consulting firm.

able and experienced public servant whose comprehensive knowledge of defense and arms control has engendered substantial confidence in Congress throughout the years." Sen. Sam Nunn, D-Ga., chairman of the Armed Services Committee, said Scowcroft's appointment "sends a very strong and positive signal about the future formulation and conduct of national security policy in the Bush administration."

One expert on national security affairs, Robert E. Hunter of the Center for Strategic and International Studies, said Scowcroft met the basic criteria for security advisers: "He has a strong strategic sense—he can fit the apples and oranges of international affairs together—and he has a passion to make the system work." Morton M. Kondracke of the *New Republic* wrote that Scowcroft "is known as a problem solver, not a master strategist. . . ."

In recent years, Scowcroft worked with Henry A. Kissinger, a former national security adviser and secretary of state, as vice chairman of Kissinger Associates Inc., a New York-Washington consulting firm. In 1983 after Congress turned down Reagan's first two proposals for basing the controversial MX intercontinental ballistic missile (ICBM), Scowcroft had headed a White House advisory panel to recommend a strategically sound and politically viable method for deploying the weapon.

In November 1986 Reagan named Scowcroft as one of three members of a "special review board," headed by ex-Sen. John Tower of Texas, to investigate White House operations in the Iran-contra affair. The Tower commission's report, issued the following February, was a scathing denunciation of Reagan's national security apparatus. However, Scowcroft said before resuming his old post that the National Security Council staff was "in really excellent condition and it will be a joy to assume responsibility for a system which is operating as well as it is now."

John H. Sununu

The White House

Born in Havana, Cuba, July 2, 1939 . . . grew up in New York and Massachusetts, moved to New Hampshire in 1969 . . . Lebanese father was in export-import business; mother was from El Salvador . . . received bachelor's, master's, and Ph.D. degrees from Massachusetts Institute of Technology, all in mechanical engineering . . . taught at Tufts University for seventeen years; served five years as associate dean of College of Engineering; ran consulting firms . . . elected governor of New Hampshire in 1982; reelected in 1984 and 1986 . . . father of eight children.

John H. Sununu
Chief of Staff

Aside from Tower, Bush's most controversial appointment was probably that of John H. Sununu to be his White House chief of staff. This appointment did not require Senate confirmation. Sununu was regarded as a man of proven political skills but short on tact and Washington experience.

In announcing his selection on November 17, 1988, Bush said Sununu would bring to the administration a "refreshing new perspective" gained from three terms as governor of New Hampshire, as well as a background as an educator and an engineer. But others said that while Sununu was a quick study, he would need time to master the ways of Washington. Such mastery might prove crucial to White House relations with the Democratic-controlled Congress and with Republican leaders such as Sen. Robert Dole, the man Sununu helped Bush defeat in the 1988 New Hampshire presidential primary.

Sununu and Bush forged close personal ties during the campaign, when the governor crisscrossed the country on Bush's behalf. The forty-nine-year-old Sununu also sported conservative credentials that helped placate right-wingers, many of whom were suspicious that Bush's sympathies—unlike Reagan's—lay with moderate elements of the party. "John Sununu is easily more conservative than any of Ronald Reagan's chiefs of staff," said Sen. Gordon J. Humphrey, R-N.H.

Citing Bush's broad foreign policy experience, Sununu told reporters that he would largely restrict his own policy advice to domestic matters, such as child care and the budget. Ironically, though, a foreign policy issue presented Sununu's first controversy. Jewish leaders criticized his refusal, alone among governors, to sign a 1986 proclamation condemning a United Nations resolution equating Zionism with racism. Sununu is of Lebanese descent and had been active in Arab-American issues. In response, he said that he opposed the resolution but felt it was inappropriate for governors to involve themselves in foreign policy.

Also greeting Sununu were concerns that his take-charge personality was all too reminiscent of Donald T. Regan. Regan, who succeeded Baker as Reagan's chief of staff, was widely disliked in Congress, and finally was forced to resign. As assessed by Robert Craig, a political science professor at the University of New Hampshire, Sununu's "big problem will be personal relationships. He's very intelligent but also very arrogant."

"Delegation will be a test for John," said New Hampshire Republican Chuck Douglas, a former state Supreme Court justice newly elected to Congress. "He has not had to delegate in little New Hampshire." Nor, Douglas added, had Sununu had to work closely with state Democrats, since Republicans dominated the Legislature.

Rep. Tony Coelho of California, the Democratic House whip, took issue with such reports. He said he had come to know Sununu during the presidential election campaign and found him self-confident but not abrasive or arrogant, and not without a sense of humor. Asked by reporters about his hot temper, Sununu displayed some of that wit: "I'm a pussycat," he replied.

As for partisanship, Bush noted that Sununu had dealt widely with Democrats as the 1987-88 chairman of the National Governors' Association.

Sununu was no stranger to authority. At age seventeen, according to a *New England Monthly* profile, he oversaw student life as the highest-ranking cadet at LaSalle Military Academy in New York. His political career took somewhat longer to get off the ground. Before he became governor, his only elective office was a single two-year term in the New Hampshire house of representatives. Most of his professional life was spent as a teacher and administrator at Tufts University in Massachusetts. He holds a Ph.D. in engineering. As governor, he became known for his mastery of financial details and his fierce support for the controversial Seabrook nuclear power plant.

William H. Webster

Teresa Zabala

Born in St. Louis March 6, 1924 ... A.B. from Amherst College in 1947 and law degree from Washington University in St. Louis, 1949 ... practiced law in Missouri, 1949-50, 1952-59, and 1961-70 ... U.S. attorney for eastern Missouri in 1960-61, and federal judge of that district in 1970-73 ... elevated to U.S. Court of Appeals for the Eighth Circuit in 1973 ... appointed director of the Federal Bureau of Investigation by President Jimmy Carter in 1978 ... named director of central intelligence by President Ronald Reagan in 1987, and reappointed by President Bush ... married, with three children.

William H. Webster
CIA Director

The reappointment of William H. Webster as director of central intelligence was expected, but controversial. Bush's aides had signaled after the election that the president-elect intended to keep Webster in office at least for a few months as a demonstration of continuity—and to make the point that Central Intelligence Agency directors should not be changed with each new president. As CIA director in 1976, Bush himself had been dumped when Jimmy Carter captured the White House from Gerald Ford.

Some conservatives and former intelligence operatives had lobbied for Webster's ouster. They complained, among other things, that the director spent too little time on the job and had downgraded the CIA's covert operations overseas.

Webster also incurred the wrath of many current and former intelligence personnel when he took strong disciplinary action against agency officials who had been involved in the secret White House network that supplied illegal military aid to the Nicaraguan contras in 1984-86.

But in 1987 Webster had been questioned about his failure as FBI director to act on early evidence of a link between aid to the contras and arms sales to Iran. The questions at Webster's CIA confirmation hearings concerned bank fraud involving an Iranian, later convicted, who posed as a Saudi Arabian prince.

Bush said that the director should provide information and advice to the president but should not be a formulator of policy. Webster's predecessor, William J. Casey, played a major role in deciding U.S. policy in several regions of the world, especially Central America. Bush said he and Webster "are in total accord" that the director "should not be in the policy business, but be in the intelligence business, and these lines can be very, very clear."

Before becoming central intelligence director, Webster was director of the Federal Bureau of Investigation for nine years. Prior to that, he served as a federal district court judge in St. Louis and then in the federal appellate court.

Appendix

Inaugural Address

Following is the text of President Bush's inaugural address, delivered January 20, 1989:

Mr. Chief Justice, Mr. President, Vice President Quayle, Senator Mitchell, Speaker Wright, Senator Dole, Congressman Michel, and fellow citizens, neighbors and friends.

There is a man here who has earned a lasting place in our hearts—and in our history. President Reagan, on behalf of our nation I thank you for the wonderful things that you have done for America.

I have just repeated word-for-word the oath taken by George Washington 200 years ago; and the Bible on which I placed my hand is the Bible on which he placed his.

It is right that the memory of Washington be with us today, not only because this is our Bicentennial Inauguration, but because Washington remains the father of our country. And he would, I think, be gladdened by this day. For today is the concrete expression of a stunning fact: Our continuity these 200 years since our government began.

We meet on democracy's front porch. A good place to talk as neighbors, and as friends. For this is a day when our nation is made whole, when our differences, for a moment, are suspended.

And my first act as President is a prayer and I ask you to bow your heads:

"Heavenly Father, we bow our heads and thank you for your love. Accept our thanks for the peace that yields this day and the shared faith that makes its continuance likely. Make us strong to do your work, willing to heed and hear your will, and write on our hearts these words: 'Use power to help people.' For we are given power not to advance our own purposes, nor to make a great show in the world, nor a name. There is but one just use of power, and it is to serve people. Help us to remember, Lord. Amen."

I come before you and assume the presidency at a moment rich with promise. We live in a peaceful, prosperous time, but we can make it better.

For a new breeze is blowing, and a world refreshed by freedom seems reborn; for in man's heart, if not in fact, the day of the dictator is over. The totalitarian era is passing, its old ideas blown away like leaves from an ancient lifeless tree.

A new breeze is blowing—and a nation refreshed by freedom stands ready to push on: There is new ground to be broken, and new action to be taken.

There are times when the future seems thick as a fog; you sit and wait, hoping the mists will lift and reveal the right path.

A Door to Tomorrow

But this is a time when the future seems a door you can walk right through—into a room called Tomorrow.

Great nations of the world are moving toward democracy—through the door to freedom.

Men and women of the world move toward free markets—through the door to prosperity.

The people of the world agitate for free expression and free thought—through the door to the moral and intellectual satisfactions that only liberty allows.

We know what works: Freedom works. We know what's right: Freedom is right. We know how to secure a more just and prosperous life for man on earth: through free markets, free speech, free elections, and the exercise of free will unhampered by the state.

For the first time in this century—for the first time in perhaps all history—man does not have to invent a system by which to live. We don't have to talk into the night about which form of government is better. We don't have to wrest justice from the kings—we only have to summon it from within ourselves.

We must act on what we know. I take as my guide the hope of a saint: In crucial things, unity—in important things, diversity—in all things, generosity.

America today is a proud, free nation, decent and civil—a place we cannot help but love. We know in our hearts, not loudly and proudly, but as a simple fact, that this country has meaning beyond what we see, and that our strength is a force for good.

But have we changed as a nation even in our time? Are we enthralled with material things, less appreciative of the nobility of work and sacrifice?

My friends, we are not the sum of our possessions. They are not the measure of our lives. In our hearts we know what matters. We cannot hope only to leave our children a bigger car, a bigger bank account. We must hope to give them a sense of what it means to be a loyal friend, a loving parent, a citizen who leaves his home, his neighborhood and town better than he found it.

And what do we want the men and women who work with us to say when we are no longer there? That we were more driven to succeed than anyone around us? Or that we stopped to ask if a sick child had gotten better, and stayed a moment there to trade a word of friendship.

No President, no government, can teach us to remember what is best in what we are. But if the man you have chosen to lead this government can help make a difference; if he can celebrate the quieter, deeper successes that are made not of gold and silk, but of better hearts and finer souls; if he can do these things, then he must.

A Kinder, Gentler Nation

America is never wholly herself unless she is engaged in high moral principle. We as a people have such a purpose today. It is to make kinder the face of the nation and gentler the face of the world.

My friends, we have work to do. There are the homeless, lost and roaming—there are the children who have nothing, no love, no normalcy—there are those who cannot free themselves of enslavement to whatever addiction—drugs, welfare, the demoralization that rules the slums. There is crime to be conquered, the rough crime of the streets. There are young women to be helped who are about to become mothers of children they can't care for and might not love. They need our care, our guidance, and our education; though we bless them for choosing life.

The old solution, the old way, was to think that public money alone could end these problems. But we have learned that that is not so. And in any case, our funds are low. We have a deficit to bring down. We have more will than wallet; but will is what we need.

We will make the hard choices, looking at what we have, perhaps allocating it differently, making our decisions based on honest need and prudent safety.

And then we will do the wisest thing of all: We will turn to the only resource we have that in times of need always grows: the goodness and the courage of the American people.

And I am speaking of a new engagement in the lives of others—a new activism, hands-on and involved, that gets the job done. We must bring in the generations, harnessing the unused talent of the elderly and the unfocused energy of the young. For not only leadership is passed from generation to generation, but so is stewardship. And the generation born after the Second World War has come of age.

I have spoken of a thousand points of light—of all the community organizations that are spread like stars throughout the nation, doing good.

We will work hand in hand, encouraging, sometimes leading, sometimes being led, rewarding. We will work on this in the White House, in the Cabinet agencies. I will go to the people and the programs that are the brighter points of light, and I will ask every member of my government to become involved.

The old ideas are new again because they're not old, they are timeless: duty, sacrifice, commitment, and a patriotism that finds its expression in taking part and pitching in.

We need a new engagement, too, between the Executive and the Congress.

An Offered Hand

The challenges before us will be thrashed out with the House and Senate.

We must bring the federal budget into balance. And we must ensure that America stands before the world united: strong, at peace, and fiscally sound. But, of course, things may be difficult.

We need compromise; we've had dissension. We need harmony; we've had a chorus of discordant voices.

For Congress, too, has changed in our time. There has grown a certain divisiveness. We have seen the hard looks and heard the statements in which not each other's ideas are challenged, but each other's motives. And our great parties have too often been far apart and untrusting of each other.

It's been this way since Vietnam. That war cleaves us still. But, friends, that war began in earnest a quarter of a century ago; and surely the statute of limitations has been reached. This is a fact: The final lesson of Vietnam is that no great nation can long afford to be sundered by a memory.

A new breeze is blowing—and the old bipartisanship must be made new again.

To my friends—and yes, I do mean friends—in the loyal opposition—and yes, I mean loyal: I put out my hand.

I am putting out my hand to you, Mr. Speaker.

I am putting out my hand to you, Mr. Majority Leader.

For this is the thing: This is the age of the offered hand.

And we can't turn back clocks, and I don't want to. But when our fathers were young, Mr. Speaker, our differences ended at the water's edge. And we don't wish to turn back time, but when our mothers were young, Mr. Majority Leader, the Congress and the Executive were capable of working together to produce a budget on which this nation could live. Let us negotiate soon—and hard. But in the end, let us produce.

The American people await action. They didn't send us here to bicker. They ask us to rise above the merely partisan. "In crucial things, unity"—and this, my friends, is crucial.

To the world, too, we offer new engagement and a renewed vow: We will stay strong to protect the peace. The "offered hand" is a reluctant fist; once made strong, it can be used with great effect.

There are today Americans who are held against their will in foreign lands, and Americans who are unaccounted for. Assistance can be shown here, and will be long remembered. Good will begets good will. Good faith can be a spiral that endlessly moves on.

"Great nations like great men must keep their word." When America says something, America means it, whether a treaty or an agreement or a vow made on marble steps. We will always try to speak clearly, for candor is a compliment. But subtlety, too, is good and has its place.

While keeping our alliances and friendships around the world strong, ever strong, we will continue the new closeness with the Soviet Union, consistent both with our security and with progress. One might say that our new relationship in part reflects the triumph of hope and strength over experience. But hope is good. And so is strength. And vigilance.

Here today are tens of thousands of our citizens who feel the understandable satisfaction of those who have taken part in democracy and seen their hopes fulfilled.

But my thoughts have been turning the past few days to those who would be watching at home—

To an older fellow who will throw a salute by himself when the flag goes by, and the woman who will tell her sons the words of the battle hymns. I don't mean this to be sentimental. I mean that on days like this, we remember that we are all part of a continuum, inescapably connected by the ties that bind —

Our children are watching in schools throughout our great land. And to them I say, thank you for watching democracy's big day. For democracy belongs to us all, and freedom is like a beautiful kite that can go higher and higher with the breeze. . . .

And to all I say: No matter what your circumstances or where you are, you are part of this day, you are part of the life of our great nation.

A President is neither prince nor pope, and I don't seek "a window on men's souls." In fact, I yearn for a greater tolerance, an easy-goingness about each other's attitudes and way of life.

Drug 'Scourge'

There are few clear areas in which we as a society must rise up united and express our intolerance. And the most obvious now is drugs. And when that first cocaine was smuggled in on a ship, it may as well have been a deadly bacteria, so much has it hurt the body, the soul of our country. There is much to be done and to be said, but take my word for it: This scourge will stop.

And so, there is much to do; and tomorrow the work begins.

And I do not mistrust the future; I do not fear what is ahead. For our problems are large, but our heart is larger. Our challenges are great, but our will is greater. And if our flaws are endless, God's love is truly boundless.

Some see leadership as high drama, and the sound of trumpets calling. And sometimes it is that. But I see history as a book with many pages—and each day we fill a page with acts of hopefulness and meaning.

The new breeze blows, a page turns, the story unfolds—and so today a chapter begins: a small and stately story of unity, diversity, and generosity—shared, and written, together.

Thank you.

God bless you.

And God bless the United States of America.

Budget Address to Congress

President Bush addressed a joint session of Congress on February 9, 1989, explaining his proposals for the fiscal 1990 budget. Following is the text of the president's address:

Less than three weeks ago, I joined you on the West Front of this very building and—looking over the monuments to our proud past—offered you my hand in filling the next page of American history with a story of extended prosperity and continued peace. Tonight, I am back, to offer you my plans as well. The hand remains extended, the sleeves are rolled up, America is waiting, and now we must produce. Together, we can build a better America.

It is comforting to return to this historic Chamber. Here, 22 years ago, I first raised my hand to be sworn into public life. So tonight, I feel as if I am returning home to friends. And I intend, in the months and years to come, to give you what friends deserve: frankness, respect, and my best judgment about ways to improve America's future.

In return, I ask for an honest commitment to our common mission of progress. If we seize the opportunities on the road before us, there will be praise enough for all. The people didn't send us here to bicker. It's time to govern.

Many Presidents have come to this Chamber in times of great crisis. War. Depression. Loss of national spirit.

Eight years ago, I sat in that chair as President Reagan spoke of punishing inflation and devastatingly high interest rates, people out of work, American confidence on the wane. Our challenge is different.

We are fortunate—a much changed landscape lies before us tonight. So I don't propose to reverse direction. We are headed the right way. But we cannot rest. We are a people whose energy and drive have fueled our rise to greatness. We are a forward-looking Nation—generous, yes, but ambitious as well—not for ourselves, but for the world. Complacency is not in our character—not before, not now, not ever.

So tonight, we must take a strong America—and make it even better. We must address some very real problems. We must establish some very clear priorities. And we must make a very substantial cut in the Federal budget deficit.

Some people find that agenda impossible. But I am presenting to you tonight a realistic plan for tackling it. My plan has four broad features: attention to urgent priorities, investment in the future, an attack on the deficit, and no new taxes.

This budget represents my best judgment of how we can address our priorities, consistent with the people's view. There are many areas in which we would all like to spend more than I propose, but we cannot until we get our fiscal house in order.

Next year alone, thanks to economic growth, without any change in the law, the Federal Government will take in over $80 billion more than it does this year. That's right—over $80 billion in new revenues, with no increase in taxes. Our job is to allocate those new resources wisely.

We can afford to increase spending—by a modest amount, but enough to invest in key priorities and still cut the deficit by almost 40 percent in one year. That will allow us to meet the targets set forth in the Gramm-Rudman-Hollings law.

But to do that, we must recognize that growth above inflation in Federal programs is not preordained, that not all spending initiatives were designed to be immortal.

I make this pledge tonight. My team and I are ready to work with the Congress, to form a special leadership group, to negotiate in good faith, to work day and night—if that's what it takes—to meet the budget targets, and to produce a budget on time.

We cannot settle for business as usual.

Government by Continuing Resolution—or government by crisis—will not do.

I ask the Congress tonight to approve several measures which will make budgeting more sensible. We could save time and improve efficiency by enacting two-year budgets. Forty-three Governors have the line-item veto. Presidents should have it, too.

At the very least, when a President proposes to rescind Federal spending, the Congress should be required to vote on that proposal—instead of killing it by inaction.

And I ask for Congress to honor the public's wishes by passing a constitutional amendment to require a balanced budget. Such an amendment, once phased in, will discipline both Congress and the Executive branch.

Several principles describe the kind of America I hope to build with your help in the years ahead.

We will not have the luxury of taking the easy, spendthrift approach to solving problems—because higher spending and higher taxes put economic growth at risk.

Economic growth provides jobs and hope. Economic growth enables us to pay for social programs. Economic growth enhances the security of the Nation. And low tax rates create economic growth.

I believe in giving Americans greater freedom and greater choice—and I will work for choice for American families, whether in the housing in which they live, the schools to which they send their children, or the child care they select for their young.

I believe that we have an obligation to those in need, but that Government should not be the provider of first resort for things that the private sector can produce better.

I believe in a society that is free from discrimination and bigotry of any kind. I will work to knock down the barriers left by past discrimination, and to build a more tolerant society that will stop such barriers from ever being built again.

I believe that family and faith represent the moral compass of the Nation—and I will work to make them strong, for as Benjamin Franklin said: "If a sparrow cannot fall to the ground without His notice, [can] a [great Nation] rise without His aid?"

And I believe in giving people the power to make their own lives better through growth and opportunity. Together, let's put power in the hands of people.

Three weeks ago, we celebrated the Bicentennial Inaugural, the 200th anniversary of the first Presidency. And if you look back, one thing is so striking about the way the Founding Fathers looked at America. They didn't talk about themselves. They talked about posterity. They talked about the future.

We, too, must think in terms bigger than ourselves.

'A Better Tomorrow'

We must take actions today that will ensure a better tomorrow. We must extend American leadership in technology, increase long-term investment, improve our education system, and boost productivity. These are the keys to building a better future.

Here are some of my recommendations:

• I propose almost $2.2 billion for the National Science Foundation to promote basic research;

• I propose to make permanent the tax credit for research and development;

• I have asked Vice President Quayle to chair a new Task Force on Competitiveness;

• I request funding for NASA and a strong space program—an increase of almost $2.4 billion over the current fiscal year. We must have a manned space station; a vigorous, safe space shuttle program; and more commercial development in space. The space program should always go "full throttle up"—that's not just our ambition; it's our destiny.

I propose that we cut the maximum tax rate on capital gains to increase long-term investment. History is clear: This will increase revenues, help savings, and create new jobs.

We won't be competitive if we leave whole sectors of America behind. This is the year we should finally enact urban enterprise zones, and bring hope to our inner cities.

Education: Top Priority

But the most important competitiveness program of all is one which improves education in America. When some of our students actually have trouble locating America on a map of the world, it is time for us to map a new approach to education.

We must reward excellence, and cut through bureaucracy. We must help those schools that need help most. We must give choice to parents, students, teachers, and principals. And we must hold all concerned accountable. In education, we cannot tolerate mediocrity.

I want to cut the drop-out rate, and make America a more literate Nation. Because what it really comes down to is this: The longer our graduation lines are today, the shorter our unemployment lines will be tomorrow.

So tonight I am proposing the following initiatives:

● the beginning of a $500-million program to reward America's best schools—"merit schools";

● the creation of special Presidential awards for the best teachers in every State—because excellence should be rewarded;

● the establishment of a new program of National Science Scholars, one each year for every Member of the House and Senate, to give this generation of students a special incentive to excel in science and mathematics;

● the expanded use of magnet schools which give families and students greater choice;

● and a new program to encourage "alternative certification"—which will let talented people from all fields teach in the classroom.

I have said I'd like to be "the Education President." Tonight, I ask you to join me by becoming "the Education Congress."

War on Drugs

Just last week, as I settled into this new office, I received a letter from a mother in Pennsylvania, who had been struck by my message in the Inaugural address. "Not 12 hours before," she wrote, "my husband and I received word that [our] son was addicted to cocaine. [He] had the world at his feet. Bright, gifted, personable . . . he could have done anything with his life. [Now] he has chosen cocaine."

"Please," she wrote, "find a way to curb the supply of cocaine. Get tough with the pushers. [Our son] needs your help."

My friends, that voice crying out for help could be the voice of your own neighbor. Your own friend. Your own son. Over 23 million Americans used illegal drugs last year—at a staggering cost to our Nation's well-being.

Let this be recorded as the time when America rose up and said "No" to drugs. The scourge of drugs must be stopped. I am asking tonight for an increase of almost a billion dollars in budget outlays to escalate the war against drugs. The war will be waged on all fronts.

Our new "Drug Czar," Bill Bennett, and I will be shoulder to shoulder leading the charge.

Some money will be used to expand treatment to the poor, and to young mothers. This will offer the helping hand to the many innocent victims of drugs—like the thousands of babies born addicted, or with AIDS, because of the mother's addiction.

Some will be used to cut the waiting time for treatment. Some money will be devoted to those urban schools where the emergency is now the worst. And much of it will be used to protect our borders, with help from the Coast Guard, the Customs Service, the departments of State and Justice, and yes, the U.S. military.

I mean to get tough on the drug criminals. Let me be clear: This President will back up those who put their lives on the line every day—our local police officers.

My budget asks for beefed-up prosecution, for a new attack on organized crime, and for enforcement of tough sentences—and for the worst kingpins, that means the death penalty.

I also want to make sure that when a drug dealer is convicted, there is a cell waiting for him. He should not go free because prisons are too full.

Let the word go out: If you are caught and convicted, you will do time.

But for all we do in law enforcement, in interdiction and treatment, we will never win this war on drugs unless we stop demand for drugs.

So some of this increase will be used to educate the young about the dangers of drugs. We must involve parents. We must involve teachers. We must involve communities. And my friends, we must involve ourselves.

One problem related to drug use demands our urgent attention and our continuing compassion. That is the terrible tragedy of AIDS. I am asking for $1.6 billion for education to prevent the disease—and for research to find a cure.

Environmental Protection

If we're to protect our future, we need a new attitude about the environment. We must protect the air we breathe. I will send to you shortly legislation for a new, more effective Clean Air Act. It will include a plan to reduce, by date certain, the emissions which cause acid rain—because the time for study alone has passed, and the time for action is now.

We must make use of clean coal. My budget contains full funding, on schedule, for the clean-coal technology agreement we have made with Canada. We intend to honor that agreement.

We must not neglect our parks. So I am asking to fund new acquisitions under the land and water conservation fund.

We must protect our oceans. I support new penalties against those who would dump medical waste and other trash in the oceans. The age of the needle on the beach must end.

In some cases, the gulfs and oceans off our shores hold the promise of oil and gas reserves which can make our Nation more secure and less dependent on foreign oil. When those with the most promise can be tapped safely, as with much of the Alaska National Wildlife Refuge, we should proceed. But we must use caution and we must respect the environment.

So tonight I am calling for the indefinite postponement of three lease sales which have raised troubling questions—two off the coast of California, and one which could threaten the Everglades in Florida. Action on these three lease sales will await the conclusions of a special task force set up to measure the potential for environmental damage.

I am directing the Attorney General and the Administrator of the Environmental Protection Agency to use every tool at their disposal to speed and toughen the enforcement of our laws against toxic waste dumpers. I want faster cleanups and tougher enforcement of penalties against polluters.

A Compassionate Society

In addition to caring for our future, we must care for those around us. A decent society shows compassion for the young, the elderly, the vulnerable, and the poor.

Our first obligation is to the most vulnerable—infants, poor mothers, children living in poverty—and my proposed budget recognizes this. I ask for full funding of Medicaid—an increase of over $3 billion—and an expansion of the program to include coverage of pregnant women who are near the poverty line.

I believe we should help working families cope with the burden of child care. Our help should be aimed at those who need it most—low-income families with young children. I support a new child care tax credit that will aim our efforts at exactly those families—without discriminating against mothers who choose to stay at home.

Now, I know there are competing proposals. But remember this: The overwhelming majority of all preschool child care is now provided by relatives and neighbors, churches and community groups. Families who choose these options should remain eligible for help. Parents should have choice.

And for those children who are unwanted or abused, or whose parents are deceased, I believe we should encourage adoption. I propose to re-enact the tax deduction for adoption expenses, and to double it to $3,000. Let's make it easier for these kids to have parents who love them.

We have a moral contract with our senior citizens. In this budget, Social Security is fully funded, including a full cost-of-living adjustment. We must honor our contract.

We must care about those in "the shadows of life," and I, like many Americans, am deeply troubled by the plight of the homeless. The causes of homelessness are many, the history is long, but the moral imperative to act is clear.

Thanks to the deep well of generosity in this great land, many organizations already contribute. But we in Government cannot stand on the sidelines. In my budget, I ask for greater support for emergency food and shelter, for health services and

measures to prevent substance abuse, and for clinics for the mentally ill—and I propose a new initiative involving the full range of Government agencies. We must confront this national shame.

There is another issue I decided to mention here tonight. I have long believed that the people of Puerto Rico should have the right to determine their own political future. Personally, I favor statehood. But I ask the Congress to take the necessary steps to let the people decide in a referendum.

Certain problems, the result of decades of unwise practices, threaten the health and security of our people. Left unattended, they will only get worse—but we can act now to put them behind us.

Earlier this week, I announced my support for a plan to restore the financial and moral integrity of our savings system. I ask Congress to enact our reform proposals within 45 days. We must not let this situation fester.

Certainly, the savings of Americans must remain secure—insured depositors will continue to be fully protected. But any plan to refinance the system must be accompanied by major reform. Our proposals will prevent such a crisis from recurring. The best answer is to make sure that a mess like this will never happen again.

The majority of thrifts in communities across this Nation have been honest; they have played a major role in helping families achieve the American dream of home ownership. But make no mistake: Those who are corrupt, those who break the law, must be kicked out of the business; and they should go to jail.

We face a massive task in cleaning up the waste left from decades of environmental neglect at America's nuclear weapons plants. Clearly, we must modernize these plants and operate them safely. That is not at issue—our national security depends on it.

But beyond that, we must clean up the

old mess that's been left behind—and I propose in this budget to more than double our current effort to do so. This will allow us to identify the exact nature of the various problems so we can clean them up—and clean them up we will.

The Defense Budget

We have been fortunate during these past eight years. America is a stronger Nation today than it was in 1980. Morale in our Armed Forces is restored. Our resolve has been shown. Our readiness has been improved. And we are at peace. There can no longer be any doubt that peace has been made more secure through strength. When America is stronger, the world is safer.

Most people don't realize that after the successful restoration of our strength, the Pentagon budget has actually been reduced in real terms for each of the last four years. We cannot tolerate further reductions.

In light of the compelling need to reduce the deficit, however, I support a one-year freeze in the military budget—something I proposed last fall in my flexible freeze plan.

This freeze will apply for only one year—after that increases above inflation will be required. I will not sacrifice American preparedness; and I will not compromise American strength.

I should be clear on the conditions attached to my recommendation for the coming year:

• the savings must be allocated to those priorities for investing in our future that I have spoken about tonight;

• this defense freeze must be part of a comprehensive budget agreement which meets the targets spelled out in the Gramm-Rudman-Hollings law without raising taxes, and which incorporates reforms in the budget process.

I have directed the National Security Council to review our national security and defense policies and report back to me within 90 days to ensure that our capabilities and resources meet our commitments and strategies.

I am also charging the Department of Defense with the task of developing a plan to improve the defense procurement process and management of the Pentagon—one which will fully implement the Packard Commission report. Many of the changes can only be made with the participation of the Congress—so I ask for your help.

We need fewer regulations. We need less bureaucracy. We need multi-year procurement and two-year budgeting. And frankly, we need less congressional micromanagement of our Nation's military policy.

America and the World

Securing a more peaceful world is perhaps the most important priority I'd like to address tonight. We meet at a time of extraordinary hope. Never before in this century have our values of freedom, democracy, and economic opportunity been such a powerful political and intellectual force around the globe.

Never before has our leadership been so crucial, because while America has its eyes on the future, the world has its eyes on America.

It is a time of great change in the world—and especially in the Soviet Union. Prudence and common sense dictate that we try to understand the full meaning of the change going on there, review our policies carefully, and proceed with caution. But I have personally assured General Secretary Gorbachev that, at the conclusion of such a review, we will be ready to move forward. We will not miss any opportunity to work for peace.

The fundamental fact remains that the Soviets retain a very powerful military machine, in the service of objectives which are still too often in conflict with ours. So let us take the new openness seriously. Let us step forward to negotiate. But let us also be realistic. And let us always be strong.

There are some pressing issues we must address: I will vigorously pursue the Strategic Defense Initiative. The spread and even use of sophisticated weaponry threatens global stability as never before.

Chemical weapons must be banned from the face of the Earth, never to be used again. This won't be easy. Verification will be difficult. But civilization and human decency demand that we try.

And the spread of nuclear weapons must be stopped. I will work to strengthen the hand of the International Atomic Energy Agency. Our diplomacy must work every day against the proliferation of nuclear weapons.

And, around the globe, we must continue to be freedom's best friend. We must stand firm for self-determination and democracy in Central America—including in Nicaragua. For when people are given the chance, they inevitably will choose a free press, freedom of worship, and certifiably free and fair elections.

We must strengthen the alliance of industrial democracies—as solid a force for peace as the world has ever known. This is an alliance forged by the power of our ideals, not the pettiness of our differences. So let us lift our sights—to rise above fighting about beef hormones to building a better future, to move from protectionism to progress.

I have asked the Secretary of State to visit Europe next week and to consult with them on the wide range of challenges and opportunities we face together—including East-West relations. And I look forward to meeting with our NATO partners in the near future.

I, too, shall begin a trip shortly—to the far reaches of the Pacific Basin, where the winds of democracy are creating new hope, and the power of free markets is unleashing a new force.

When I served as our representative in China just 14 years ago, few would have predicted the scope of the changes we've witnessed since then. But in preparing for this trip, I was struck by something I came across from a Chinese writer. He was speaking of his country, decades ago—but his words speak to each of us, in America, tonight.

"Today," he said, "we are afraid of the simple words like goodness and mercy and kindness."

My friends, if we're to succeed as a Nation, we must rediscover those words.

In just three days, we mark the birthday of Abraham Lincoln—the man who saved our Union, and gave new meaning to the word opportunity. Lincoln once said: "I hold that while man exists, it is his duty to improve not only his own condition, but to assist in ameliorating [that of] mankind."

It is this broader mission to which I call all Americans. Because the definition of a successful life must include serving others.

To the young people of America, who sometimes feel left out—I ask you tonight to give us the benefit of your talent and energy through a new program called "YES," for Youth Entering Service to America.

To those men and women in business—remember the ultimate end of your work—to make a better product, to create better lives. I ask you to plan for the longer term and avoid the temptation of quick and easy paper profits.

To the brave men and women who wear the uniform of the United States of America—thank you. Your calling is a high one—to be the defenders of freedom and the guarantors of liberty. And I want you to know that the Nation is grateful for your service.

To the farmers of America, we appreciate the bounty you provide. We will work with you to open foreign markets to American agricultural products.

To the parents of America, I ask you to get involved in your child's schooling. Check on their homework. Go to school, meet the teachers, care about what is happening there. It is not only your child's future on the line, it is America's.

To kids in our cities—don't give up hope. Say no to drugs. Stay in school. And yes, "Keep hope alive."

To those 37 million Americans with some form of disability—you belong in the economic mainstream. We need your talents in America's work force. Disabled Americans must become full partners in America's opportunity society.

To the families of America watching tonight in your living rooms: Hold fast to your dreams, because ultimately America's future rests in your hands.

And to my friends in this Chamber, I ask for your cooperation to keep America growing while cutting the deficit. That is only fair to those who now have no vote— the generations to come.

Let them look back and say that we had the foresight to understand that a time of peace and prosperity is not a time to rest, but a time to push forward. A time to invest in the future.

And let all Americans remember that no problem of human making is too great to be overcome by human ingenuity, human energy, and the untiring hope of the human spirit. I believe this. I would not have asked to be your President if I didn't.

Reaching Out to Congress

Tomorrow, the debate on the plan I have put forward begins. I ask the Congress to come forward with your proposals, if they are different. Let us not question each other's motives. Let us debate. Let us negotiate. But let us solve the problem.

Recalling anniversaries may not be my specialty in speeches . . . but tonight is one of some note. On February 9, 1941, just 48 years ago tonight, Sir Winston Churchill took to the airwaves during Britain's hour of peril.

He had received from President Roosevelt a hand-carried letter quoting Longfellow's famous poem: "Sail on, O Ship of State! Sail on, Oh Union, strong and great! Humanity with all its fears, with all the hopes of future years, Is hanging breathless on thy fate!"

Churchill responded on this night by radio broadcast to a nation at war, but he directed his words to Roosevelt. "We shall not fail or falter," he said. "We shall not weaken or tire. Give us the tools, and we will finish the job."

Tonight, almost a half-century later, our peril may be less immediate, but the need for perseverance and clear-sighted fortitude is just as great.

Now, as then, there are those who say it can't be done. There are voices who say that America's best days have passed. That we are bound by constraints, threatened by problems, surrounded by troubles which limit our ability to hope.

Well, tonight I remain full of hope. We Americans have only begun on our mission of goodness and greatness. And to those timid souls, I repeat the plea —give us the tools; and we will do the job.

Thank you, and God bless you, and God bless America.

Nomination Acceptance Speech

Following is the text of Vice President George Bush's speech at the Republican National Convention in New Orleans, August 18, 1988, formally accepting the party's presidential nomination:

Thank you ladies and gentlemen, thank you very, very much.

I have many friends to thank tonight. I thank the voters who supported me. I thank the gallant men who entered the contest for this presidency this year, and who've honored me with their support. And, for their kind and stirring words, I thank Governor Tom Kean of New Jersey, Senator, Senator Phil Gramm of Texas, President Gerald Ford—and my friend, and my friend, President Ronald Reagan.

I accept your nomination for president. I mean to run hard, to fight hard, to stand on the issues—and I mean to win.

There are a lot, there are a lot of great stories in politics about the underdog winning—and this is going to be one of them.

And we're going to win with the help of Senator Dan Quayle of Indiana—a young leader who has become a forceful voice in preparing America's workers for the labor force of the future. What a superb job he did here tonight.

Born in the middle of the century, in the middle of America, and holding the promise of the future—I'm proud to have Dan Quayle at my side.

Many of you have asked, many of you have asked, "When will this campaign really begin?" Well, I've come to this hall to tell you, and to tell America: Tonight is the night.

For seven and a half years I've helped the president conduct the most difficult job on Earth. Ronald Reagan asked for, and received, my candor. He never asked for, but he did receive, my loyalty. And those of you who saw the president's speech last week, and listened to the simple truth of his words, will understand my loyalty all these years.

And now, now you must see me for what I am: the Republican candidate for president of the United States. And now I turn to the American people to share my hopes and intentions, and why and where I wish to lead.

And so tonight is for big things. But I'll try to be fair to the other side. I'll try to hold my charisma in check.

I reject the temptation to engage in personal references. My approach this evening is, as Sergeant Joe Friday used to say, "Just the facts, ma'am."

And after all, after all, the facts are on our side.

Build a Better America

I seek the presidency for a single purpose, a purpose that has motivated millions of Americans across the years and the ocean voyages. I seek the presidency to build a better America. It's that simple—and that big.

I'm a man who sees life in terms of missions—missions defined and missions completed.

And when I was a torpedo bomber pilot they defined the mission for us. And before we took off, we all understood that no matter what, you try to reach the target. And there have been other missions for me—Congress, and China, the CIA. But I'm here tonight, and I am your candidate, because the most important work of my life is to complete the mission we started in 1980. And how, and how do we complete it? We build on it.

The stakes are high this year and the choice is crucial, for the differences between the two candidates are as deep and wide as they have ever been in our long history.

Not only two very different men, but two very different ideas of the future will be voted on this Election Day.

And what it all comes down to is this: My opponent's view of the world sees a long slow decline for our country, an inevitable fall mandated by impersonal historical forces.

But America is not in decline. America is a rising nation.

He sees, he sees America as another pleasant country on the U.N. [United Nations] roll call, somewhere between Albania and Zimbabwe. And I see America as the leader—a unique nation with a special role in the world.

And this has been called the American century, because in it we were the dominant force for good in the world. We saved Europe, cured polio, went to the moon, and lit the world with our culture. And now we are on the verge of a new century, and what country's name will it bear? I say it will be another American century.

Our work is not done, our force is not spent.

'We Can Deliver'

There are those, there are those who say there isn't much of a difference this year. But America, don't let 'em fool ya.

Two parties this year ask for your support. Both will speak of growth and peace. But only one has proved it can deliver. Two parties this year ask for your trust, but only one has earned it.

Eight years ago, eight years ago, I stood here with Ronald Reagan and we promised, together, to break with the past and return America to her greatness. Eight years later, look at what the American people have produced: the highest level of economic growth in our entire history—and the lowest level of world tensions in more than 50 years.

You know, some say this isn't an election about ideology, but it's an election about competence. Well, it's nice of them to want to play on our field. But this election isn't only about competence, for competence is a narrow ideal.

Competence makes the trains run on time but doesn't know where they're going. Competence, competence is the creed of the technocrat who makes sure the gears mesh but doesn't for a second understand the magic of the machine.

The truth is, the truth is, this election is about the beliefs we share, the values we honor and the principles we hold dear.

But, but since someone brought up competence . . .

Consider the size of our triumph: A record number of Americans at work, a record high percentage of our people with jobs, a record high of new businesses, a high rate of new businesses, a record high rate of real personal income.

These are facts.

And one way, and one way we know our opponents know the facts is that to attack our record they have to misrepresent it. They call it a Swiss cheese economy. Well, that's the way it may look to the three blind mice.

But, but when they were in charge it was all holes and no cheese.

Inflation—you know the litany—inflation was 13 percent when we came in. We got it down to four. Interest rates, interest rates were more than 21. We cut them in half. Unemployment, unemployment was up and climbing, and now it's the lowest in 14 years.

My friends, eight years ago this economy was flat on its back—intensive care. And we came in and gave it emergency treatment: Got the temperature down by lowering regulation, and got the blood pressure down when we lowered taxes. And pretty soon the patient was up, back on his feet, and stronger than ever.

And now who do we hear knocking on the door but the same doctors who made him sick. And they're telling us to put them in charge of the case again? My friends, they're lucky we don't hit 'em with a malpractice suit!

More Jobs: Economic Power

We've created 17 million new jobs [in] the past five years—more than twice as many as Europe and Japan combined. And they're good jobs. The majority of them created in the past six years paid an average—average—of more than $22,000 a year. And someone better take a message to Michael: Tell him, tell him that we have been creating good jobs at good wages. The fact is, they talk and we deliver.

They promise and we perform.

And there are millions of young Americans in their 20s who barely remember, who barely remember the days of gas lines and unemployment lines. And now they're marrying and starting careers. To those young people I say, "You have the opportunity you deserve, and I'm not going to let them take it away from you."

The leaders, the leaders of the expansion have been the women of America who helped create the new jobs, and filled two out of every three of them. And to the women of America I say, "You know better than anyone that equality begins with economic empowerment. You're gaining economic power, and I'm not going to let them take it away from you."

There are millions, there are millions of older Americans who were brutalized by inflation. We arrested it—and we're not going to let it out on furlough.

We're going, and we're going to keep the Social Security trust fund sound, and out of reach of the big spenders. To America's elderly I say, "Once again you have the security that is your right, and I'm not going to let them take it away from you."

I know the liberal Democrats are worried about the economy. They're worried it's going to remain strong. And they're right, it is—with the right leadership it will remain strong.

But let's be frank. Things aren't perfect in this country. There are people who haven't tasted the fruits of the expansion. I've talked to farmers about the bills they can't pay and I've been to the factories that feel the strain of change. And I've seen the urban children who play amidst the shattered glass and the shattered lives. And, you know, there are the homeless. And you know, it doesn't do any good to debate endlessly which policy mistake of the '70s is responsible. They're there, and we have to

help them.

But what we must remember if we're to be responsible and compassionate is that economic growth is the key to our endeavors.

I want growth that stays, that broadens, and that touches, finally, all Americans, from the hollows of Kentucky to the sunlit streets of Denver, from the suburbs of Chicago to the broad avenues of New York, and from the oil fields of Oklahoma to the farms of the Great Plains.

And can we do it? Of course we can. We know how. We've done it. If we, if we continue to grow at our current rate, we will be able to produce 30 million jobs in the next eight years.

And we will do it—by maintaining our commitment to free and fair trade, by keeping government spending down, and by keeping taxes down.

Peace Through Strength

Our economic life is not the only test of our success. One issue overwhelms all the others, and that is the issue of peace.

Look at the world on this bright August night. The spirit of democracy is sweeping the Pacific rim. China feels the winds of change. New democracies assert themselves in South America. And one by one the unfree places fall, not to the force of arms but to the force of an idea: freedom works.

And we, we have a new relationship with the Soviet Union. The INF [intermediate-range nuclear-force] treaty, the beginning of the Soviet withdrawal from Afghanistan, the beginning of the end of the Soviet proxy war in Angola, and with it the independence of Namibia. Iran and Iraq move toward peace.

It's a watershed. It is no accident.

It happened when we acted on the ancient knowledge that strength and clarity lead to peace—weakness and ambivalence lead to war. You see, you see, weakness tempts aggressors. Strength stops them. I will not allow this country to be made weak again—never.

The tremors in the Soviet world continue. The hard earth there has not yet settled. Perhaps what is happening will change our world forever. And perhaps not. A prudent skepticism is in order. And so is hope.

But either way, we're in an unprecedented position to change the nature of our relationship. Not by preemptive concession, but by keeping our strength. Not by yielding up defense systems with nothing won in return, but by hard, cool engagement in the tug and pull of diplomacy.

My life, my life has been lived in the shadow of war—I almost lost my life in one.

And I hate war. Love peace.

And we have peace.

And I am not going to let anyone take it away from us.

Our economy is stronger but not invulnerable, and the peace is broad but can be broken. And now we must decide. We will surely have change this year, but will it be change that moves us forward? Or change that risks retreat?

In 1940, when I was barely more than a boy, Franklin Roosevelt said we shouldn't change horses in midstream.

My friends, these days the world moves even more quickly, and now, after two great terms, a switch will be made. But when you have to change horses in midstream, doesn't it make sense to switch to one who's going the same way?

Family and Community

An election that is about ideas and values is also about philosophy. And I have one.

At the bright center is the individual. And radiating out from him or her is the family, the essential unit of closeness and of love. For it is the family that communicates to our children—to the 21st century—our culture, our religious faith, our traditions and history.

From the individual to the family to the community, and then on out to the town, the church and the school, and, still echoing out, to the county, the state, and the nation—each doing only what it does well, and no more. And I believe that power must always be kept close to the individual, close to the hands that raise the family and run the home.

I am guided by certain traditions. One is that there is a God and he is good, and his love, while free, has a self-imposed cost: We must be good to one another.

I believe in another tradition that is, by now, imbedded in the national soul. It is that learning is good in and of itself. You know, the mothers of the Jewish ghettoes of the east would pour honey on a book so the children would know that learning is sweet. And the parents who settled hungry Kansas would take their children in from the fields when a teacher came. That is our history.

And there is another tradition. And that is the idea of community—a beautiful word with a big meaning. Though liberal Democrats have an odd view of it. They see "community" as a limited cluster of interest groups, locked in odd conformity. And in this view, the country waits passive while Washington sets the rules.

But that's not what community means—not to me.

For we are a nation of communities, of thousands and tens of thousands of ethnic, religious, social, business, labor union, neighborhood, regional and other organizations—all of them varied, voluntary and unique.

This is America: the Knights of Columbus, the Grange, Hadassah, the Disabled American Veterans, the Order of AHEPA [American Hellenic Educational Progressive Association], the Business and Professional Women of America, the union hall, the Bible study group, LULAC [League of

United Latin American Citizens], "Holy Name"—a brilliant diversity spread like stars, like a thousand points of light in a broad and peaceful sky.

Does government have a place? Yes. Government is part of the nation of communities—not the whole, just a part.

And I don't hate government. A government that remembers that the people are its master is a good and needed thing.

'Old-Fashioned Common Sense'

I respect old-fashioned common sense, and have no great love, and I have no great love for the imaginings of the social planners. You see, I like what's been tested and found to be true.

For instance.

Should public school teachers be required to lead our children in the pledge of allegiance? My opponent says no—and I say yes.

Should society be allowed to impose the death penalty on those who commit crimes of extraordinary cruelty and violence? My opponent says no—but I say yes.

And should our children, should our children have the right to say a voluntary prayer, or even observe a moment of silence in the schools? My opponent says no—but I say yes.

And should free men and women have the right to own a gun to protect their home? My opponent says no—but I say yes.

And is it right to believe in the sanctity of life and protect the lives of innocent children? My opponent says no—but I say yes.

You see, we must, we must change, we've got to change from abortion to adoption. And let me tell you this: Barbara and I have an adopted granddaughter. And the day of her christening we wept with joy. I thank God that her parents chose life.

I'm the one who believes it is a scandal to give a weekend furlough to a hardened first-degree killer who hasn't even served enough time to be eligible for parole.

I'm the one who says a drug dealer who is responsible for the death of a policeman should be subject to capital punishment.

Policies for the Future

And I'm the one who will not raise taxes. My opponent now says, my opponent now says he'll raise them as a last resort, or a third resort. Well, when a politician talks like that, you know that's one resort he'll be checking into. And, my opponent won't rule out raising taxes. But I will.

And the Congress will push me to raise taxes, and I'll say no, and they'll push, and I'll say no, and they'll push again. And I'll say to them: Read my lips. No new taxes.

Let me tell you more—let me tell you more, let me just tell you more about the mission.

On jobs, my mission is: 30 in 8. Thirty million jobs in the next eight years.

Every one of our children deserves a first-rate school. The liberal Democrats want power in the hands of the federal government. And I want power in the hands of the parents. And, I will—and I will, I will encourage merit schools. I will give more kids a head start. And I'll make it easier to save for college.

I want a drug-free America—and this will not be easy to achieve. But I want to enlist the help of some people who are rarely included. Tonight I challenge the young people of our country to shut down the drug dealers around the world. Unite with us, work with us.

"Zero tolerance" isn't just a policy, it's an attitude. Tell them what you think of people who underwrite the dealers who put poison in our society. And while you're doing that, my administration will be telling the dealers: Whatever we have to do we'll do, but your day is over, you're history.

I am going to do whatever it takes to make sure the disabled are included in the mainstream. For too long they've been left out. But they're not going to be left out anymore.

And I am going to stop ocean dumping. Our beaches should not be garbage dumps and our harbors should not be cesspools.

And I am going to have the FBI trace the medical wastes and we are going to punish the people who dump those infected needles into our oceans, lakes and rivers. And we must clean the air. We must reduce the harm done by acid rain.

And I will put incentives back into the domestic energy industry, for I know from personal experience there is no security for the United States in further dependence on foreign oil.

In foreign affairs I will continue our policy of peace through strength. I will move toward further cuts in strategic and conventional arsenals of both the United States and the Soviet Union and the Eastern Bloc and NATO. I will modernize and preserve our technological edge and that includes strategic defense.

And a priority, a priority: Ban chemical and biological weapons from the face of the Earth. That will be a priority with me.

And I intend to speak for freedom, stand for freedom, be a patient friend to anyone, East or West, who will fight for freedom.

A New Harmony

It seems to me the presidency provides an incomparable opportunity for "gentle persuasion."

And I hope to stand for a new harmony, a greater tolerance. We've come far, but I think we need a new harmony among the races in our country. And we're on a journey into a new century, and we've got to leave that tired old baggage of bigotry behind.

Some people who are enjoying our prosperity have forgotten what it's for. But they diminish our triumph when they act as if wealth is an end in itself.

And there are those who have dropped their standards along the way, as if ethics were too heavy and slowed their rise to the top. There's graft in city hall, and there's greed on Wall Street; there's influence peddling in Washington, and the small corruptions of everyday ambition.

But you see, I believe public service is honorable. And every time I hear that someone has breached the public trust it breaks my heart.

And I wonder sometimes if we have forgotten who we are. But we're the people who sundered a nation rather than allow a sin called slavery—and we're the people who rose from the ghettoes and the deserts.

And we weren't saints, but we lived by standards. We celebrated the individual, but we weren't self-centered. We were practical, but we didn't live only for material things. We believed in getting ahead, but blind ambition wasn't our way.

The fact is prosperity has a purpose. It is to allow us to pursue "the better angels," to give us time to think and grow. Prosperity with a purpose means taking your idealism and making it concrete by certain acts of goodness.

It means helping a child from an unhappy home learn how to read—and I thank my wife Barbara for all her work in helping people to read and all her work for literacy in this country.

It means teaching troubled children through your presence that there is such a thing as reliable love. Some would say it's soft and insufficiently tough to care about these things. But where is it written that we must act as if we do not care, as if we are not moved?

Well, I am moved. I want a kinder and gentler nation.

'Quiet Man'

Two men this year ask for your support. And you must know us.

As for me, I have held high office and

done the work of democracy day by day. Yes, my parents were prosperous; and their children sure were lucky. But there were lessons we had to learn about life.

John Kennedy discovered poverty when he campaigned in West Virginia; there were children who had no milk. And young Teddy Roosevelt met the new America when he roamed the immigrant streets of New York. And I learned a few things about life in a place called Texas.

And when I—and when I was, when I was working on this part of the speech, Barbara came in and asked what I was doing. And I looked up, and I said I'm working hard. And she said: "Oh dear, don't worry, relax, sit back, take off your shoes and put up your silver foot."

Now, we moved to West Texas 40 years ago—40 years ago this year. The war was over, and we wanted to get out and make it on our own. Those were exciting days. We lived in a little shotgun house, one room for the three of us. Worked in the oil business, and then started my own.

And in time we had six children. Moved from the shotgun to a duplex apartment to a house. And lived the dream—high school football on Friday nights, Little League, neighborhood barbecue.

People don't see their own experience as symbolic of an era—but of course we were.

And so was everyone else who was taking a chance and pushing into unknown territory with kids and a dog and a car.

But the big thing I learned is the satisfaction of creating jobs, which meant creating opportunity, which meant happy families, who in turn could do more to help others and enhance their own lives.

I learned that the good done by a single good job can be felt in ways you can't imagine.

It's been said that I'm not the most compelling speaker, and there are actually those who claim that I don't always communicate in the clearest, most concise way. But I dare them to keep it up—go ahead: Make my 24-hour time period!

Well, I—I may be, may not be the most eloquent, but I learned that, early on, that eloquence won't draw oil from the ground.

And I may sometimes be a little awkward. But there's nothing self-conscious in my love of country.

And I am a quiet man, but—I am a quiet man, but I hear the quiet people others don't. The ones who raise the family, pay the taxes, meet the mortgages.

And I hear them and I am moved, and their concerns are mine.

Man with a Mission

A president must be many things.

He must be a shrewd protector of America's interests; and he must be an idealist who leads those who move for a freer and more democratic planet.

And he must see to it that government intrudes as little as possible in the lives of the people; and yet remember that it is right and proper that a nation's leader take an interest in the nation's character.

And he must be able to define—and lead—a mission.

For 7½ years, I have worked with a great president—I have seen what crosses that big desk. I have seen the unexpected crisis that arrives in a cable in a young aide's hand. And I have seen problems that simmer on for decades and suddenly demand resolution. And I have seen modest decisions made with anguish, and crucial decisions made with dispatch.

And so I know that what it all comes down to, this election—what it all comes down to, after all the shouting and the cheers—is the man at the desk. And who should sit at that desk.

My friends, I am that man.

I say it, I say it without boast or bravado.

I've fought for my country, I've served, I've built—and I will go from the hills to the hollows, from the cities to the suburbs to the loneliest town on the quietest street to take our message of hope and growth for every American to every American.

I will keep America moving forward, always forward, for a better America, for an endless enduring dream and a thousand points of light.

This is my mission. And I will complete it.

Thank you.

You know, you know it is customary to end an address with a pledge or a saying that holds a special meaning. And I've chosen one that we all know by heart. One that we all learned in school. And I ask everyone in this great hall to stand and join me in this—we all know it.

I pledge allegiance to the flag of the United States of America and to the republic for which it stands, one nation under God, indivisible, with liberty and justice for all.

Thank you.

Where They Voted . . . and Where They Didn't
(1988 presidential-election turnout as percentage of voting-age population)

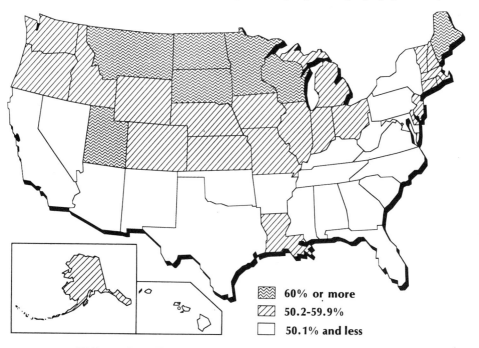

60% or more

50.2-59.9%

50.1% and less

	'88 Turnout Rate (as percentage of voting-age pop.)	Change, '84-'88 (in percentage points)			'88 Turnout Rate (as percentage of voting-age pop.)	Change, '84-'88 (in percentage points)
NATIONAL	50.1%	−3.0	26. Alaska		51.7	−7.5
1. Minnesota	66.3	−1.9	27. Louisiana		51.3	−3.2
2. Montana	62.4	−2.7	28. Delaware		51.0	−4.4
3. Maine	62.2	−2.6	29. Wyoming		50.3	−3.0
4. Wisconsin	62.0	−1.5	30. Pennsylvania		50.1	−3.9
5. North Dakota	61.5	−1.2	31. Mississippi		49.9	−2.3
South Dakota	61.5	−1.0	32. Maryland		49.1	−2.3
7. Utah	60.0	−1.6	33. Oklahoma		48.7	−3.4
8. Iowa	59.3	−2.9	34. Kentucky		48.2	−2.6
9. Vermont	59.1	−0.7	Virginia		48.2	−2.5
10. Oregon	58.6	−3.2	36. New York		48.1	−3.1
11. Idaho	58.3	−1.6	37. California		47.4	−2.2
12. Massachusetts	58.1	+0.5	38. New Mexico		47.3	−4.0
13. Connecticut	57.9	−3.2	39. Arkansas		47.0	−4.8
14. Nebraska	56.8	+1.2	40. West Virginia		46.7	−5.0
15. Colorado	55.1	0.0	41. Alabama		45.8	−4.1
Ohio	55.1	−2.9	42. Arizona		45.0	−0.2
17. Missouri	54.8	−2.5	43. Nevada		44.9	+3.4
18. New Hampshire	54.7	+1.7	44. Florida		44.7	−3.5
19. Washington	54.6	−3.8	Tennessee		44.7	−4.4
20. Kansas	54.3	−2.5	46. Texas		44.2	−3.0
21. Michigan	54.0	−3.9	47. North Carolina		43.4	−4.0
22. Illinois	53.3	−3.8	48. Hawaii		43.0	−1.3
Indiana	53.3	−2.6	49. District of Columbia		39.4	−3.8
24. Rhode Island	53.0	−2.8	50. South Carolina		38.9	−1.8
25. New Jersey	52.1	−4.5	51. Georgia		38.8	−3.2

Index